LITTLE LATIN
READERS

LITTLE LATIN READERS
Workbook

Liber Primus
PUELLA RŌMĀNA
(The Roman Girl)

Julie A. Collorafi

www.littlelatinreaders.com

www.littlelatinreaders.com

TABLE OF CONTENTS

FIRST DECLENSION NOUNS

(Read p. 2-3 in reader.)

● **NOUNS:** **Nouns** are words which name *persons, places, things and ideas.* Some English **common** nouns are *girl, boy, house,* and *church.* Common **nouns** denote a class of objects or a concept.

▶ *Latin nouns are placed in groups called declensions.*

● **FIRST DECLENSION NOUNS:** First declension nouns are Latin nouns which end in **-a** in the nominative singular case. We will only study first declension nouns in this reader.

puella
girl

Learn
these two first
declension
common nouns.

fēmina
woman

Do you see the -a at the end of each of these Latin words?

▶*The -a at the end of these Latin nouns is a sign that these nouns belong to the first declension.*

There are no Latin words for **a, an** or **the**, so these must be added to the Latin nouns when they are translated to English. For the Latin noun **puella,** you may say **a girl,** or **the girl**. Circle the **-a** at the end of each noun below:

puella   **fēmina**

A. GRAMMAR QUESTIONS (Circle the correct word in the parentheses which best completes the sentence.)

1. (**Nouns / Adjectives**) are words that name persons, places, things or ideas.

2. Latin **nouns** are placed in groups called (**verbs / declensions**).

3. (**First / Second**) declension nouns are Latin nouns which end in **-a** in the nominative singular case.

B. IDENTIFICATION (Write the Latin nouns in the correct boxes.)

C. MATCHING (Draw a line from the Latin noun to its translation.)

1. **puella**   woman

2. **fēmina**   girl

D. ENGLISH-TO-LATIN (Write the Latin noun for each word.)

1. **girl** _____

2. **woman** _____

2

E. ECCLESIASTICAL LATIN VOWELS PRONUNCIATION
Say the vowel sounds found in ecclesiastical (Church) Latin below:

a   "ah" as in *father*
æ   in between "eh" and "ay"
e   "eh" as in *met*
i   "ee" as in *feet*
o   "oh" as in *only*
u   "oo" as in *suit*
œ   "ay" as in *ray*

F. LATIN VOWELS PRACTICE (Match the vowels and sounds.)
1. **o sounds like** _____"oh"_____.
2. **i sounds like** _____.
3. **a sounds like** _____.
4. **e sounds like** _____.
5. **u sounds like** _____.
6. **æ sounds like** _____.
7. **œ sounds like** _____.

G. ECCLESIASTICAL LATIN CONSONANTS PRONUNCIATION
Say the consonant sounds found in ecclesiastical (Church) Latin below:

c	before e, i, y, æ, or œ	like "ch" in *chant*
c	before a, o, or u	like "k" in *car*
g	before a, o, or u	like "g" in *gone*
g	before e, i, y, or ae	like "g" in *generation*
gn	before a, or, or u	like "ny" in *Bunyan*
s	between two vowels	like "z" as in *zebra*
ti	before a vowel	like "tsee"

3

✎ **H. Latin Consonants Practice** (Match the consonants and sounds.)

1. *gn* before a, or, or u **sounds like** _____.
2. *c* before e, i, y, æ, or œ **sounds like** _____.
3. *s* between two vowels **sounds like** _____.
4. *ti* before a vowel **sounds like** _____.
5. *c* before a, o, or u **sounds like** _____.
6. *g* before e, i, y, or ae **sounds like** _____.

✎ **I. First Declension Nouns Practice** (Read the following first declension nouns and their definitions. Circle the -a at the end of each noun. The macron, the — horizontal line over the long vowels, indicate that those vowel sounds are long and should be lengthened or drawn out slightly.) Write each word.

aquā (ah/kwah) *water*   *aqua* _____

anima (ah/nee/mah) *soul* _____

āra (ar/ah) *altar* _____

columna (coh/loom/nah) *column* _____

cuppa (coo/pah) *cup* _____

furca (fur/cah) *fork* _____

fama (fah/mah) *fame, reputation* _____

gemma (jem/mah *gem, jewel* _____

viola (vee/oh/lah) *violet* _____

lūna (loo/nah) *moon* _____

rota (ro/tah) *wheel* _____

tabula (tah/boo/lah) *tablet* _____

mūsica (moo/see/kah) *music* _____

vacca (vahk/cah) *cow* _____

fabula (fah/boo/lah) *story, fable* _____

flāmma (flam/mah) *flame* _____

urna (ur/nah) *urn* _____

4

The Being Verb Est

(Read p. 4-5 in reader.)

- **Using Est:** **Est** is a **being verb** and is like the English being verb *is*. **Est** is a **singular** verb, meaning it is used with a **singular** subject and can be translated as *he is, she is,* or *it is.*

Est puella.
She is a girl.

- **Singular Subject:** If the subject is **singular**, it is **one** person, place or thing. If the subject is **plural**, it is **more than one** person, place or thing. **Est** is used only with singular subjects.

▶ *The subject is the person, place or thing the sentence is about.*

🖊 **A. English Practice** (Write the subject of each sentence. Is the subject singular or plural?)

1. **The boy is tall.** _____boy_____ singular or plural
2. **Rome is a city.** _____ singular or plural
3. **The geese fly.** _____ singular or plural
4. **The lake is blue.** _____ singular or plural
5. **The boys run.** _____ singular or plural
6. **Roses are red.** _____ singular or plural
7. **Ann sings.** _____ singular or plural
8. **Stars twinkle.** _____ singular or plural

- **The Adverb Nōn:** **Nōn** is a particle and is used as an adverb to negate verbs, adjectives, nouns, or phrases. (**Lūcia** in the sentence below is a **proper noun,** a name used for a specific person, place, thing, or idea, spelled with an initial capital letter.)

Lūcia nōn est ancilla.
Lucia is not a maidservant.

A. New Vocabulary Practice (Write each.)

ancilla, -æ, f. *maidservant* _____

fēmina, -æ, f. *woman* _____

puella, -æ, f. *girl* _____

nōn *not* _____

B. Grammar Questions (Circle the correct word in the parentheses.)

1. The (**subject / verb**) is the person, place, or thing a sentence is about

2. A **subject** is (**singular / plural**) if it is **one** person, place or thing.

3. A **subject** is (**singular / plural**) if it is **more than one** person, place or thing.

4. **Est** is a (**being / transitive**) verb.

5. **Est** is a (**singular / plural**) being verb.

6. (**Nouns / Adjectives**) are words that name persons, places or things.

7. Latin nouns are placed in groups called (**declensions / conjugations**).

8. (**First / Second**) declension nouns are Latin nouns which end in **-a** in the nominative singular case.

9. A (**proper / common**) noun denotes a class of objects.

10. A (**proper / common**) noun names a specific person, place, thing, or idea, spelled with a beginning capital letter.

C. Latin Practice (Circle the best translation of each sentence.)

1. **Nōn est fēmina.**   a. She is not a woman.   b. The girl is good.
2. **Est ancilla.**   a. Portia prays.   b. She is a maidservant.
3. **Lūcia est puella.**   a. The girl is Maria.   b. Lucy is a girl.
4. **Maria est fēmina.**   a. Maria is a woman.   b. Lucy is good.

D. English-to-Latin (Write the Latin word for each English word.)

1. **girl** _____

2. **woman** _____

3. **maidservant** _____

✎ E. SUBJECT-VERB AGREEMENT (If the subject is singular, the verb must be singular; if the subject is plural, the verb must be plural. Circle the correct form of the being verb below. Is the verb singular or plural?

1. The moon (is / are) full.	singular	plural
2. The stars (is / are) shining.	singular	plural
3. The sun (is / are) bright.	singular	plural
4. There (is / are) eight planets.	singular	plural
5. Mercury (is / are) closest to the sun.	singular	plural
6. The sun (is / are) a star.	singular	plural
7. A meteor (is / are) a rocky object in space.	singular	plural
8. Earth (is / are) the third planet from the sun.	singular	plural

✎ F. PROPER AND COMMON NOUNS (Is the underlined noun proper or common?)

1. <u>Lūcia</u> nōn est fēmina.	proper	common
2. <u>Ancilla</u> est Maria.	proper	common
3. <u>Maria</u> est fēmina.	proper	common
4. <u>Fēmina</u> nōn est Maria.	proper	common
5. <u>Puella</u> nōn est Lūcia.	proper	common

✎ G. MISSING MACRONS (Place macrons (‒) where needed.)

1. puella
2. femina
3. ancilla
4. Maria
5. Lucia
6. non

✎ H. PROOFREADING (Draw a line through the spelling errors ane write on lines.)

1. Lūcia nōn est ~~ancila~~.   *ancilla* _____
2. Eit fēmina. _____
3. Maria est fæmina. _____
4. Nōn est pueela. _____
5. Puella nūon est Maria. _____
6. Fēmina est Lūcie. _____

I. NAME THE PICTURE (Match each picture with an appropriate Latin noun.)

1. _____   2. _____   3. _____

J. ENGLISH-TO-LATIN (Compose a Latin sentence for each.)

1. **She is a woman.**

_____

2. **She is a maidservant.**

_____

3. **She is a girl.**

_____

4. **She is not a maidservant.**

_____

5. **She is not a girl.**

_____

6. **She is not a woman.**

_____

7. **Lucia is a girl.**

_____

8. **Maria is a woman.**

_____

9. **Lucia is not a maidservant.**

_____

10. **Maria is not a girl.**

_____

FIRST DECLENSION ADJECTIVES

(Read p. 6-7 in the reader.)

Puella est Rōmāna.

- **ADJECTIVES:** In the English sentence below the subject is underlined and the adjective is circled:

The <u>house</u> is (large.)

subject   adjective

▶ *An adjective is a word that describes a noun or pronoun.*

In these Latin sentences, the subjects are followed by adjectives:

<u>Fēmina</u> est (Rōmāna.) *The woman is Roman.*

<u>Lūcia</u> est (bona.) *Lucy is good.*

Est (pulchra.) *She is pretty.*

✎ **NEW ADJECTIVES TO LEARN** (Write on line.)
bona *good*
Christiāna *Christian*
opulenta *wealthy*
parva *small*
pulchra *pretty, beautiful*
Rōmāna *Roman*
longa *long*

✎ **PROPER NOUNS** (Write on line.)
Claudia, -æ, f.
Lūcia, -æ, f.
Portia, -æ, f.
Octāvia, -æ, f.

9

✎ **A. Subject /Adjective Identification** (Underline the subject and circle the adjective in each sentence.)

1. **Fēmina est pulchra.**
2. **Lūcia est Rōmāna.**
3. **Puella nōn est opulenta.**
4. **Octāvia est Christiāna.**
5. **Ancilla est bona.**

✎ **B. Grammar Questions** (Choose the correct word to complete the sentence.)

1. An (**adjective / noun**) is a word which describes a noun or pronoun.

2. The (**subject / verb**) is the person, place, or thing a sentence is about.

3. A **subejct** is (**singular / plural**) if it is **one** person, place or thing.

4. A **subject** is (**singular / plural**) if it is **more than one.**

5. **Est** is a (**singular / plural**) being verb.

6. (**Adjectives / Nouns**) are words that name persons, places or things.

7. Latin nouns are placed in groups called (**declensions / conjugations**).

8. (**First / Second**) declension nouns end in **-a** in the nominative singular.

9. A (**proper / common**) noun denotes a class of objects.

10. A (**proper / common**) noun names a specific person, place, thing, or idea, spelled with a beginning capital letter.

✎ **C. Matching Sentences** (Match each with its correct translation.)

____1. **Fēmina est bona.**   a. **She is Roman.**
____2. **Puella nōn est pulchra.**   b. **The woman is good.**
____3. **Est Rōmāna.**   c. **The woman is pretty.**
____4. **Fēmina est pulchra.**   d. **She is wealthy.**
____5. **Puella est Rōmāna.**   e. **The girl is Roman.**
____6. **Est opulenta.**   f. **She is small.**
____7. **Fēmina nōn est Christiāna.** g. **The woman is not Christian.**
____8. **Est parva.**   h. **The maid servant is good.**
____9. **Ancilla est bona.**   i. **The girl is not pretty.**

✏️ **D. ADJECTIVES PRACTICE** (Fill in the blank with a nominative singular feminine adjective listed on p. 9.)

1. **Octāvia est** _____.
2. **Puella est** _____.
3. **Claudia est** _____.
4. **Ancilla nōn est** _____.
5. **Lūcia est** _____.
6. **Fēmina nōn est** _____.
7. **Maria est** _____.
8. **Puella nōn est** _____.

✏️ **E. SUBJECTS** (Fill in the blank with a nominative singular first declension feminine noun.)

1. _____ **est pulchra.**
2. _____ **nōn est opulenta.**
3. _____ **est Christiāna.**
4. _____ **est bona.**
5. _____ **nōn est Rōmāna.**
6. _____ **nōn est parva.**
7. _____ **est opulenta.**

✏️ **F. SUBJECT/ADJECTIVE IDENTIFICATION** (Is the underlined word the subject of the sentence or an adjective describing the subject?)

1. <u>**Fēmina**</u> **est opulenta.**	subject	adjective
2. <u>**Lūcia**</u> **est pulchra.**	subject	adjective
3. **Puella est** <u>**Christiāna.**</u>	subject	adjective
4. <u>**Octāvia**</u> **nōn est Rōmāna.**	subject	adjective
5. **Ancilla est** <u>**bona.**</u>	subject	adjective
6. **Puella est** <u>**pulchra.**</u>	subject	adjective
7. **Lūcia est** <u>**Rōmāna.**</u>	subject	adjective
8. <u>**Ancilla**</u> **est Christiāna.**	subject	adjective

G. TRUE OR FALSE? (Read each statement and write **True** or **False**.)

_____ 1. If the subject of a sentence is singular, the verb must be singular.

_____ 2. An adjective is a word that names a person, place or thing.

_____ 3. Est is a singular being verb.

_____ 4. The subject is the person, place or thing the sentence is about.

_____ 5. First declension nouns end in -w in the nominative singular.

_____ 6. Latin nouns are placed in groups called declensions.

_____ 7. A subject is singular if it is three persons, places or things.

_____ 8. A proper noun names a specific person, place, thing, or idea, spelled with a beginning capital letter.

H. MISSING MACRONS (Place the macron (—) where needed.)

1. **bona**
2. **pulchra**
3. **Christiana**
4. **Romana**
5. **Lucia**
6. **opulenta**
7. **non**

I. PROPER AND COMMON NOUNS (Identify each noun as proper or common.)

1. **Claudia**	(proper)	**common**
2. **puella**	proper	**common**
3. **fēmina**	proper	**common**
4. **Lūcia**	proper	**common**
5. **Maria**	proper	**common**
6. **ancilla**	proper	**common**
7. **Octāvia**	proper	**common**
8. **Portia**	proper	**common**

12

FIRST DECLENSION PLURAL NOUNS
(Read p. 8-9 in the reader.)

▶*A singular noun refers to one person, place or thing.*

▶*A plural noun refers to more than one person, place, or thing.*

	SINGULAR	PLURAL
	dog	dog**s**
	girl	girl**s**
	boy	boy**s**
	chair	chair**s**
	box	box**es**

English plural nouns are usually formed by adding -s or -es to a singular noun.

puellæ

● FIRST DECLENSION PLURAL ENDING is made by removing the ending **-a,** and replacing it with the diphthong ending **-æ.***

SINGULAR	PLURAL
puell-a	**puell-æ**

✏ NEW LATIN NOUNS PRACTICE (Write each on the line.)

casa, -æ, f. *cottage, small house* _____

ecclēsia, -æ, f. *church* _____

familia, -æ, f. *family* _____

silva, -æ, f. *woods, forest* _____

via, -æ, f. *road, way* _____

villa, -æ, f. *villa, manor* _____

*The diphthong **-æ** combines two adjacent vowel sounds within the same syllable and is pronounced as "ay".

✎ **A. PLURAL PRACTICE** (Make these first declension nouns plural by replacing the singular ending -a with the plural ending -æ)

SINGULAR	PLURAL
1. fēmina *(woman)*	fēmin _____ *(women)*
2. puella *(girl)*	puell _____ *(girls)*
3. villa *(manors)*	vill _____ *(manors)*
4. ecclēsia *(church)*	ecclēsi _____ *(churches)*
5. via *(road)*	vi _____ *(roads)*
6. ancilla *(maid)*	ancill _____ *(maids)*
7. silva *(forest)*	silv_____ *(forests)*
8. casa *(cottage)*	cas _____ *(cottages)*
9. familia *(family)*	famili _____ *(families)*

✎ **B. SUBJECT / ADJECTIVE IDENTIFICATION** (Underline the subjects and circle the adjectives.)

1. <u>Puella</u> est (pulchra.)
2. Casa est parva.
3. Claudia est opulenta.
4. Lūcia est Christiāna.

✎ **C. PRONUNCIATION PRACTICE**

1. **Ancilla est Christiāna.** (ahn/**chee**/lah est kris/tee/**ah**/nah)
2. **Puella est pulchra.** (pooh/**el**/lah est **pool**/krah)
3. **Ancilla nōn est Rōmāna.** (ahn/**chee**/lah nohn est roh/**mah**/nah)
4. **Est opulenta.** (est (oh/pooh/**len**/tah)
5. **Casa est parva.** (**cah**/sah est **par**/vah)
6. **Ecclēsia est Christiāna.** (ay/**clay**/zee/ah est kris/tee/**ah**/nah)
7. **Via est Rōmāna.** (vee/ah est roh/**mah**/nah)
8. **Familia est Christiāna.** (fah/mee/**lee**/ah est kris/tee/**ah**/nah)

*Remember that long vowel sounds with diacritical markings (ā, ē, ī, ō, ū) are slightly lengthened or drawn out.

✎ **D. MATCHING** (Find the corect translations of these adjective phrases.)

<u>D.</u> 1. puellæ pulchræ   A. small cottage

____ 2. casa parva   B. a good maidservant

____ 3. villa opulenta   C. Roman roads

____ 4. fēminæ Christiānæ   D. the pretty girls

____ 5. ancilla bona   E. the Christian church

____ 6. viæ Rōmānæ   F. a Roman girl

____ 7. ecclēsia Christiāna   G. the opulent villa

____ 8. puella Rōmāna   H. Christian women

✎ **E. ADJECTIVE PRACTICE** (Fill in the blanks with an adjective describing the underlined nominative feminine singular subject.)

1. <u>Fēmina</u> est _____.

2. <u>Casa</u> est _____.

3. <u>Portia</u> est _____.

4. <u>Villa</u> nōn est _____.

5. <u>Lūcia</u> nōn est _____.

6. <u>Puella</u> est _____.

7. <u>Via</u> est _____.

8. <u>Silva</u> est _____.

9. <u>Ecclēsia</u> est _____.

10. <u>Ancilla</u> nōn est _____

     opulenta bona Christiāna Rōmāna parva pulchra longa

✎ **F. MISSING MACRONS** (Place the macron (−) where needed..)

1. femina

2. ecclesia

3. Christiana

4. Lucia

5. Romana

6. Octavia

✎ **G. SUBJECT/ADJECTIVE IDENTIFICATION** (Is the underlined word a subject or an adjective describing the subject?)

1. <u>Via</u> est longa.	subject	predicate adjective
2. <u>Portia</u> est pulchra.	subject	predicate adjective
3. Fēmina est <u>Rōmāna</u>.	subject	predicate adjective
4. <u>Villa</u> est opulenta.	subject	predicate adjective
5. Ancilla est <u>bona</u>.	subject	predicate adjective
6. Puella est <u>Christiāna</u>.	subject	predicate adjective
7. Maria nōn est <u>Rōmāna</u>.	subject	predicate adjective
8. <u>Silva</u> est parva.	subject	predicate adjective
9. <u>Ecclēsia</u> est Christiāna.	subject	predicate adjective
10. <u>Fēmina</u> est bona.	subject	predicate adjective

✎ **H. PROOFREADING** (Draw a line through each mistake and write the correct word on the line.)

1. Via est ~~longe.~~ _____
2. Famillia est Christiāna. _____
3. Ecclisia nōn est parva. _____
4. Nōn eest Octāvia. _____
5. Sīlvo est parva. _____
6. Villa est opullenta. _____

✎ **I. NAME THE PICTURE** (What vocabulary words best fit each picture?)

1. _____ 2. _____ 3. _____ 4. _____

LESSONS 1-4 REVIEW

PART I. CONCEPT AND VOCABULARY REVIEW

A. GRAMMAR REVIEW (Circle the correct word in the parentheses.)

1. (Singular / Plural) nouns refer to more than one person, place or thing.

2. (Singular / Plural) nouns refer to one person, place or thing

3. An (adjective / adverb) is a word which describes a noun or pronoun.

4. Est is a (singular / plural) being verb.

5. (Nouns / Verbs) are words that name persons, places or things.

6. The first declension nominative singular ending is (-a / -æ).

7. The first declension nominative plural ending is (-a / -æ).

8. Latin nouns are placed in groups called (declensions / conjugations).

9. Most first declension nouns are (feminine / masculine.)

10. The (subject / verb) is the person, place or thing the sentence is about.

11. Nōn is an (adverb / adjective).

B. FIRST DECLENSION NOUN REVIEW (Give English translation of each.)

1. ancilla _____

2. casa _____

3. ecclēsia _____

4. fēmina _____

5. puella _____

6. silva _____

7. via _____

8. villa _____

9. familia _____

C. ADJECTIVE REVIEW (Give English translation of each.)

1. bona _____

2. Christiāna _____

3. longa _____

4. opulenta _____

5. pulchra _____

6. Rōmāna _____

D. BEING VERBS REVIEW (Give English translation of each.)

1. est _____

2. sunt _____

17

PART II. PRACTICAL APPLICATION

E. FORMING PLURALS (Make these first declension nouns plural.)

1. fēmina _____
2. puella _____
3. villa _____
4. ecclēsia _____
5. via _____
6. ancilla _____
7. silva _____
8. casa _____
9. familia _____

F. SUBJECT / PREDICATE ADJECTIVE IDENTIFICATION (Underline the subjects and circle the predicate adjectives.)

1. <u>Fēmina</u> est (Christiāna.)
2. Casa nōn est opulenta.
3. Octāvia est Rōmāna.
4. Via est longa.
5. Claudia est pulchra.

G. SENTENCE PRACTICE (Give an English translation for each sentence.)

1. Est bona.

_____

2. Familia est opulenta.

_____

3. Portia est puella.

_____

4. Ancilla est Christiāna.

_____

5. Ecclēsia nōn est parva.

_____

18

THE BEING VERB SUNT

(Read p. 10-11 in the reader.)

- **USING SUNT:** **Sunt** is a **being verb** and is like the English being verb *are*. **Sunt** is a **plural** verb and is translated as *they are*.

Fēminæ sunt bonæ. The women are good.

- **THE CONJUNCTION ET:** **Sunt** may also be used with **compound subjects** where **two or more nouns are used as the subject.** In the following phrases, two or more nouns are joined by the conjunction *et* which means *and*.

Octavia et Lūcia

Lūcia et Maria et Claudia

fēmina et puella

- **COMPOUND SUBJECTS:** Two nouns may be used as the compound subject of a sentence and are used with a plural verb like *sunt*. When an adjective or noun is used to describe the plural subject, the adjective or noun must also be plural.

Claudia et Lūcia sunt puellæ. *Claudia and Lucy are girls.*
Puella et fēmina sunt Rōmānæ. *The girl and the woman are Roman.*

✎ **LATIN BEING VERBS PRACTICE** (Write each.)
est *he, she, it is* _____
sunt *they are* _____

19

 **A. LATIN PRACTICE** (Circle the correct verb for each sentence.)

1. Maria (est / sunt) puella.

2. Claudia (est / sunt) fēmina.

3. Ancilla (est / sunt) bona.

4. Lūcia et Octāvia (est / sunt) Rōmānæ.

5. Puellæ (est / sunt) Christiānæ.

B. NAME THE PICTURE (Circle the correct name for each picture.)

1 **a. fēminæ**
   b. fēmina

2. **a. Claudia et Octavia**
   b. fēminæ

3. **a. Lūcia et Maria**
   b. puella

4. **a. puella et fēmina**
   b. fēmina

5. **a. puella**
   b. Maria et Lūcia

6. **a. fēmina**
   b. puellæ

✎ **C. Plural Subjects** (Fill in the blank with a nominative plural subject that agrees with the verb and the adjective in each sentence.)

1. _____ sunt opulentæ.

2. _____ et _____ sunt Rōmānæ.

3. _____ sunt bonæ.

4. _____ et _____ sunt puellæ.

5. _____ sunt Christiānæ.

6. _____ sunt longæ.

7. _____ nōn sunt parvæ.

8. _____ sunt pulchræ.

Fēminæ   Ancillæ   Lūcia et Portia   Silvæ
Puellæ   Viæ   Claudia et Octāvia

✎ **D. Matching** (Find the corect translations of these adjective phrases.)

____1. casæ parvæ   A. small forest
____2. villæ opulentæ   B. a long road
____3. familia bona   C. opulent villas
____4. viæ Rōmānæ   D. a pretty woman
____5. ancilla bona   E. the Christian churches
____6. silva parva   F. Roman roads
____7. ecclēsiæ Christiānæ   G. the Roman girls
____8. puellæ Rōmānæ   H. a good family
____9. via longa   I. small cottages
____10. fēmina pulchra   J. the good maidservant

21

✎ **E. Subject/Predicate Adjective Identification** (Is the underlined word the subject or a predicate adjective describing the subject?)

1. <u>Silva</u> est parva.   subject   adjective
2. <u>Lūcia</u> est bona.   subject   adjective
3. Puella est <u>Christiana</u>.   subject   adjective
4. <u>Claudia</u> est opulenta.   subject   adjective
5. Familia non est <u>Rōmāna</u>. subject   adjective

✎ **F. Parts of Speech** (Identify each Latin word as a noun, adjective, adverb, conjunction, or being verb.)

1. casa	noun	adjective	adverb	conjunction	being verb
2. nōn	noun	adjective	adverb	conjunction	being verb
3. opulenta	noun	adjective	adverb	conjunction	being verb
4. et	noun	adjective	adverb	conjunction	being verb
5. sunt	noun	adjective	adverb	conjunction	being verb
6. parva	noun	adjective	adverb	conjunction	being verb
7. silva	noun	adjective	adverb	conjunction	being verb
8. est	noun	adjective	adverb	conjunction	being verb
9. ecclēsia	noun	adjective	adverb	conjunction	being verb
10. longa	noun	adjective	adverb	conjunction	being verb

✎ **G. English-to-Latin** (Give a Latin translation of each simple sentence.)

1. Portia is Roman.

_____

2. The family is Christian.

_____

3. Maria and Lucia are girls.

_____

4. The woman is good.

_____

5. The roads are long.

_____

6. Octavia and Claudia are women.

22

MORE WORK WITH ADJECTIVES
(Read p. 12-13 in the reader.)

puella Rōmāna

English adjectives are placed before the nouns they modify.

the **ugly** duckling
a **red** house
the **kind** bishop

In Latin, however, **adjectives of quality,** which answer the question *what kind?,* **are usually placed after the nouns they modify.** This looks strange at first, but you will soon get used to it.

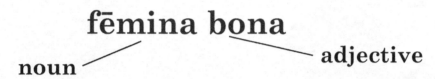

fēmina bona

noun   **adjective**

▶*Adjectives of quality usually go after the nouns they modify.*

• **THE ADVERB NŌN:** In the reading the adverb *nōn* is used, which means **not** and usually sits **before** the verb it modifies:

Nōn est Lūcia. *She is not Lucy.*

🖍 A. ADJECTIVE PRACTICE *(Circle adjectives and underline nouns.*
1. the small town
2. a good boy
3. the enormous ship
4. the magnificent cathedral
5. the yellow sun
6. a steep hill
7. the busy town
8. an ancient wall

B. LATIN PRACTICE (Circle the correct sentence for each picture.)

1. a. Fēmina est bona.
   b. Fēminæ sunt bonæ.

2. a. Puella est pulchra.
   b. Puellae sunt pulchræ.

3. a. Fēmina sunt Rōmāna.
   b. Fēminæ est Rōmānæ.

4. a. Lūcia est Rōmāna.
   b. Puellæ sunt Rōmānæ.

C. VERB PRACTICE (Do the subject and verb agree?)

1. <u>Puellæ</u> **est** bona.   Yes _____ No _____
2. <u>Fēmina</u> **est** opulenta.   Yes _____ No _____
3. <u>Lūcia</u> **sunt** Rōmāna.   Yes _____ No _____
4. <u>Lūcia et Octāvia</u> **sunt** Rōmānæ.   Yes _____ No _____
5. <u>Puella et fēmina</u> **est** bonæ.   Yes _____ No _____
6. <u>Lūcia et Portia</u> **est** bona.   Yes _____ No _____
7. <u>Fēminæ</u> **est** Christiānæ.   Yes _____ No _____
8. <u>Puella</u> **est** parva.   Yes _____ No _____

✎ **D. NOUN /ADJECTIVE IDENTIFICATION** (Is the underlined word a noun or an adjective?)

1. Est <u>ecclēsia</u> Christiāna.   noun   adjective
2. Antōnia est fēmina <u>bona</u>.   noun   adjective
3. Sunt <u>villæ</u> opulentæ.   noun   adjective
4. <u>Puella</u> Rōmāna est Claudia.   noun   adjective
5. Maria est ancilla <u>bona</u>.   noun   adjective
6. Octāvia est fēmina <u>opulenta</u>.   noun   adjective
7. Puella <u>pulchra</u> est Lūcia.   noun   adjective
8. <u>Casa</u> parva est.   noun   adjective

✎ **E. MISSING ADJECTIVES** (Fill in the blank with adjectives that agree with the underlined nouns.)

1. <u>Puella</u> _____ est Maria.
2. Claudia et Octāvia sunt <u>puellæ</u> _____.
3. Sunt <u>fēminæ</u> _____.
4. Antōnia <u>fēmina</u> _____ est.
5. Maria nōn est <u>fēmina</u> _____.
6. Sunt <u>viæ</u> _____.
7. Sunt <u>ecclēsiæ</u> _____.
8. Est <u>silva</u> _____.

✎ **F. MISSING BEING VERBS** (Fill in the blank with the being verbs (**est**, **sunt**) that agree with the underlined subjects.)

1. <u>Portia et Lūcia</u> _____ puellæ Rōmānæ.
2. <u>Claudia et Octāvia</u> _____ opulentæ.
3. <u>Puella</u> _____ bona.
4. <u>Viæ</u> _____ longæ.
5. <u>Maria</u> _____ fēmina Christiāna.
6. <u>Ecclēsiae</u> nōn _____ parvæ.
7. <u>Villa</u> _____ opulenta.

✎ **G. Proper and Common Nouns** (Identify each noun.)

1. puella   proper   common
2. Claudia   proper   common
3. ecclēsia   proper   common
4. Antōnia   proper   common
5. fēmina   proper   common
6. via   proper   common
7. casa   proper   common
8. Lūcia   proper   common
9. Maria   proper   common
10. ancilla   proper   common

✎ **H. Proofreading** (Draw a line through each spelling mistake and write the correct word on the line.)

1. Octāvia et Claudia sunt ~~pellae~~ Rōmānæ. _____

2. Antōnia est fēmna Christiāna. _____

3. Via long est. _____

4. Cassa est parva. _____

5. Eclēsiæ sunt Christiānæ. _____

6. Villa est opulentara. _____

7. Ancila est bona. _____

8. Octāvia est pulcra. _____

✎ **I. Adjective Phrases** (Translate the following English adjective phrases into Latin.)

1. a good woman _____
2. the good women _____
3. the Christian church _____
4. the Christian churches _____
5. the small cottage _____
6. small cottages _____

PREPOSITIONAL PHRASES WITH *IN*
(Read p. 14-17 in the reader.)

in villā

• **PREPOSITIONS** show relationships between words in a sentence. There are only three prepositions used in this book, *in, ad, super.*

The preposition *in* is used to show location: *in, on* or *upon.* First declension nouns used with the preposition **in** end in -ā if they are singular. Long vowel sound **ā** is lengthened or drawn out slightly.

(Learn these new prepositional phrases:)

in viā *on the road*
in ecclēsiā *in the church*
in terrā *on land*
in silvā *in the forest*
in casā *in the cottage*

A. GRAMMAR REVIEW (Circle the correct word in the parentheses.)

1. **(In / Ad)** may be translated as *in, on* or *upon.*
2. **Sunt** is a **(singular / plural)** being verb.
3. **Est** is a **(singular / plural)** being verb.
4. The first declension ending **(-æ / -a)** is plural.
5. The first declenstion ending **(-æ / -a)** is singular.
6. **Nōn** is an **(adverb / adjective)**.
7. **Et** is a **(conjunction / preposition)** which joins words together.
8. **In** is a **(conjunction / preposition)** showing relationship between words.
9. **In silvā** is a **(conjunction / prepositional phrase)**.
10. **Adjectives of quality** are usually placed **(before / after)** nouns they modify.
11. A **(proper / common)** noun denotes a class of objects.
12. A **(proper / common)** noun names a specific person, place, thing, or idea, spelled with a beginning capital letter.

B. ENGLISH PRACTICE (Circle the best translation.)

1. The women are in the country house.
   a. Fēmina est in villā.
   b. Fēminæ sunt in villā.

2. They are Christians.
   a. Maria est puella Christiāna.
   b. Sunt Christiānæ.

3. The girls are not Roman.
   a. Puella nōn est Rōmāna.
   b. Puellæ nōn sunt Rōmānæ.

C. MATCHING (Match the following phrases with the correct translations.)

_____1. puella bona   A. the Roman woman
_____2. ecclēsia pulchra   B. the pretty girl
_____3. puella pulchra   C. a wealthy woman
_____4. puella Rōmāna   D. a good girl
_____5. fēmina Rōmāna   E. a small cottage
_____6. puella Christiāna   F. a beautiful church
_____7. fēmina opulenta   G. the Christian girl
_____8. casa parva   H. a Roman girl

D. NAME THE PICTURE (Write a Latin adjective phrase for each.)

1. _____

2. _____

28

✎ **E. SUBJECT / VERB AGREEMENT** (Which being verb agrees with the underlined subject? Write **est** or **sunt** in the blank.)

1. _____ <u>puellæ</u> in viā.
2. _____ <u>femīnæ</u> in villā.
3. _____ <u>ancilla</u> in casā.
4. <u>Fēmina</u> _____ in ecclēsiā.
5. <u>Puellæ</u> _____ in silvā.

✎ **F. PARTS OF SPEECH** (Identify each Latin word as a noun, adjective, adverb, conjunction, preposition or being verb.)

1. **silva**	noun	adjective	adverb	conjunction	being verb	preposition
2. **in**	noun	adjective	adverb	conjunction	being verb	preposition
3. **pulchra**	noun	adjective	adverb	conjunction	being verb	preposition
4. **est**	noun	adjective	adverb	conjunction	being verb	preposition
5. **et**	noun	adjective	adverb	conjunction	being verb	preposition
6. **opulenta**	noun	adjective	adverb	conjunction	being verb	preposition
7. **nōn**	noun	adjective	adverb	conjunction	being verb	preposition
8. **sunt**	noun	adjective	adverb	conjunction	being verb	preposition
9. **fēmina**	noun	adjective	adverb	conjunction	being verb	preposition
10. **bona**	noun	adjective	adverb	conjunction	being verb	preposition
11. **longa**	noun	adjective	adverb	conjunction	being verb	preposition
12. **puella**	noun	adjective	adverb	conjunction	being verb	preposition
13. **parva**	noun	adjective	adverb	conjunction	being verb	preposition
14. **Portia**	noun	adjective	adverb	conjunction	being verb	preposition
15. **Rōmāna**	noun	adjective	adverb	conjunction	being verb	preposition

✎ **G. MISSING MACRONS** (Place the macrons on the ablative ending in these prepositinal phrases.)

1. **in via**
2. **in casa**
3. **in silva**
4. **in ecclesia**
5. **in villa**

29

H. NOMINATIVE ENDINGS (Fill in the missing forms of these first declension feminine nouns in the nominative case.)

	SINGULAR	PLURAL
1.	silva	
2.		ecclēsiæ
3.		viæ
4.	puella	
5.	villa	
6.		fēminæ
7.	ancilla	
8.	casa	
9.		familiæ

I. MISSING ADJECTIVES (Fill in the missing blank with an adjective that agrees with the underlined subject.)

1. <u>Portia</u> est _____.

2. <u>Claudia et Octāvia</u> sunt _____.

3. <u>Antōnia</u> est _____.

4. <u>Lūcia et Antōnia</u> sunt _____.

5. <u>Maria</u> est _____.

6. <u>Maria et Portia</u> sunt _____.

7. <u>Ecclēsia</u> est _____.

8. <u>Ecclēsiæ</u> sunt _____.

7. <u>Via</u> est _____.

8. <u>Viæ</u> sunt _____.

7. <u>Casa</u> est _____.

8. <u>Casæ</u> sunt _____.

PLURAL ADJECTIVE PHRASES
(Read p. 18-21 in the reader.)

▶ *Latin adjectives must agree with the nouns they modify
in case, number and gender.*

• **MODIFYING NOUNS:** If a Latin noun is **feminine** and **singular**, the adjective modifying it must have a **feminine** and **singular** ending. If the noun is **feminine** and **plural**, the adjective must also be **feminine** and **plural**. If the noun is in the **nominative** case, the adjective must aslo be in the **nominative** case. Examples of singular and plural adjective phrases in the nominative case:

ecclēsia splendida *splendid church*
ecclēsiæ splendidæ *splendid churches*
via antīqua *ancient road*
viæ antīquæ *ancient roads*

fēminæ Rōmānæ

✎ **NEW ADJECTIVES TO LEARN** (Write each.)

antīqua *old*	_____
longa *long*	_____
magna *large*	_____
splendida *splendid*	_____

• **THE PREPOSITION AD** The preposition *ad* is used to show *direction towards*. First declension **singular** nouns used with the preposition *ad* end in **-am.** *Ad* is translated as *to, toward.*

Learn
these new
prepositional
phrases:

ad ecclēsiam *to the church*
ad villam *to the villa*
ad silvam *to the forest*
ad casam *to the cottage*

✏ NEW INTRANSITIVE VERBS TO LEARN

In the reader, some simple verb forms are used. These are called **intransitive verbs** since they do not require an object to complete their meaning. (Write each on the line.)

ambulat *he, she, it walks* _____

cantat *he, she, it sings* _____

ōrat *he, she, it prays* _____

Ōrat.

* These verbs are third person singular verbs in the present tense.

✏ A. INTRANSITIVE VERB PRACTICE (Match each with its translation.)

____1. Ambulat.   A. The girl walks on the road.
____2. Ōrat.   B. The girl walks in the forest.
____3. In viā puella ambulat.   C. She prays.
____4. Fēmina cantat.   D. The woman sings.
____5. In silvā puella ambulat.   E. The girl walks to the church.
____6. Ad ecclēsiam puella ambulat. F. She walks.

✏ B. BEING VERB PRACTICE (Underline subjects and circle correct verbs.)

1. Ecclēsia (est / sunt) splendida.
2. Fēmina et puella (est / sunt) bonæ.
3. Octāvia et Claudia (est / sunt) opulentæ.

✏ C. ADJECTIVE PHRASE PRACTICE (Circle the best label for each.)

1. a. via antīqua   2. a. silva magna   3. a. puellæ bonæ
   b. casa parva   b. ecclēsia antīqua   b. fēmina Rōmāna
   c. villa opulenta   c. puella Christiāna   c. via longa

D. MISSING ADJECTIVES (Circle the predicate adjective which agrees in number with the underlined subject and fill in the blank.)

1. <u>Ecclēsia</u> est _____.   antīqua   antīquæ
2. <u>Viæ</u> sunt _____.   longa   longæ
3. <u>Silva</u> est _____.   magna   magnæ
4. <u>Villæ</u> sunt _____.   splendida   splendidæ
5. <u>Fēminæ</u> sunt _____.   bona   bonæ
6. <u>Casa</u> est _____.   parva   parvæ
7. <u>Puella</u> est _____.   Rōmāna   Rōmānæ
8. <u>Ancillæ</u> non sunt _____.   Rōmāna   Rōmānæ
9. <u>Familiae</u> sunt _____.   Christiāna   Christiānæ
10. <u>Octāvia</u> est _____.   opulenta   opulentæ

E. MISSING INTRANSITIVE VERBS (Fill in the blank with the intransitive verbs (ambulat, cantat, ōrat) which agree with the underlined subjects.)

1. In ecclēsiā <u>Lūcia</u> _____.
2. Ad villam <u>ancilla</u> _____.
3. <u>Fēmina</u> in viā _____.
4. In villā <u>Claudia</u> _____.
5. Ad ecclēsiam <u>puella</u> _____.
6. <u>Familia</u> in ecclēsiā _____.
7. <u>Puella</u> ad casam _____.
8. In viā <u>Antōnia</u> _____.

F. SUBJECT / VERB AGREEMENT (Do the underlined subjects and verbs agree in number? Circle the correct answer.)

1. <u>Antōnia et Maria</u> cantat.   Yes   No
2. <u>Fēmina</u> ambulat.   Yes   No
3. <u>Villæ</u> sunt splendidæ.   Yes   No
4. <u>Ecclēsia</u> est antīqua.   Yes   No
5. <u>Silvæ</u> est magnæ.   Yes   No
6. <u>Lūcia</u> ōrat.   Yes   No
7. <u>Fēmina et puella</u> ambulat.   Yes   No
8. <u>Portia</u> cantat.   Yes   No
9. <u>Casa</u> nōn sunt magna.   Yes   No
10. <u>Claudia</u> est pulchra.   Yes   No

✎ **G. MATCHING** (Match the following phrases with the correct translations.)

_____1. good girls   A. fēminæ Rōmānæ
_____2. ancient church   B. villa magna
_____3. long roads   C. viæ longæ
_____4. Roman girls   D. familiæ Christiānæ
_____5. large villa   E. ecclēsia antīqua
_____6. wealthy family   F. ecclēsiæ splendidæ
_____7. ancient road   G. via antīqua
_____8. small cottages   H. puellæ bonæ
_____9. splendid churches   I. familia opulenta
_____10. good maidservant   J. casæ parvæ
_____11. Christian families   K. puellæ Rōmānæ
_____12. Roman women   L. ancilla bona

✎ **H. PARTS OF SPEECH** (Identify each Latin word as a noun, adjective, adverb, conjunction, preposition or being verb.)

1. **ad**	noun	adjective	adverb	conjunction	being verb	intransitive verb	(preposition)
2. **fēmina**	noun	adjective	adverb	conjunction	being verb	intransitive verb	preposition
3. **ōrat**	noun	adjective	adverb	conjunction	being verb	intransitive verb	preposition
4. **est**	noun	adjective	adverb	conjunction	being verb	intransitive verb	preposition
5. **magna**	noun	adjective	adverb	conjunction	being verb	intransitive verb	preposition
6. **opulenta**	noun	adjective	adverb	conjunction	being verb	intransitive verb	preposition
7. **nōn**	noun	adjective	adverb	conjunction	being verb	intransitive verb	preposition
8. **ambulat**	noun	adjective	adverb	conjunction	being verb	intransitive verb	preposition
9. **in**	noun	adjective	adverb	conjunction	being verb	intransitive verb	preposition
10. **sunt**	noun	adjective	adverb	conjunction	being verb	intransitive verb	preposition
11. **Lūcia**	noun	adjective	adverb	conjunction	being verb	intransitive verb	preposition
12. **puella**	noun	adjective	adverb	conjunction	being verb	intransitive verb	preposition
13. **antīqua**	noun	adjective	adverb	conjunction	being verb	intransitive verb	preposition
14. **silva**	noun	adjective	adverb	conjunction	being verb	intransitive verb	preposition
15. **Rōmāna**	noun	adjective	adverb	conjunction	being verb	intransitive verb	preposition

LESSONS 5-8 REVIEW

PART I. CONCEPT AND VOCABULARY REVIEW

A. GRAMMAR REVIEW (Circle the correct word in the parentheses.)

1. (Singular / Plural) nouns refer to more than one person, place or thing.
2. (Singular / Plural) nouns refer to one person, place or thing
3. An (adjective / adverb) is a word which describes a noun or pronoun.
4. **Est** is a (singular / plural) being verb.
5. **Sunt** is a (singular / plural) being verb.
6. (Nouns / Prepositions) are words that name persons, places or things.
7. The first declension nominative **singular** ending is (-a / -æ).
8. The first declension nominative **plural** ending is (-a / -æ).
9. Latin nouns are placed in groups called (declensions / conjugations).
10. Most first declension nouns are (feminine / masculine.)
11. The (subject / preposition) is the person, place or thing the sentence is about.
12. (In / Ad) may be translated as *in, on* or *upon.*
13. **Nōn** is an (adverb / adjective).
14. **Et** is a (conjunction / preposition) which joins words together.
15. **In** is a (conjunction / preposition) showing relationship between words.
16. *In silvā* is a (conjunction / prepositional phrase.)
17. **Adjectives of quality** are usually placed (before / after) nouns they modify.
18. Latin adjectives (must / must not) agree with the nouns they modify in case, number and gender.
19. **Intransitive verbs** (do / do not) require an object to complete their meaning.
20. **Ōrat, cantat** and **ambulat** are (intransitive / being) verbs.

B. FIRST DECLENSION NOUN REVIEW (Give English translation of each.)

1. **ancilla** _____
2. **casa** _____
3. **ecclēsia** _____
4. **fēmina** _____
5. **puella** _____
6. **silva** _____
7. **via** _____
8. **villa** _____

C. ADJECTIVE REVIEW (Give English translation of each.)
1. antīqua _____
2. bona _____
3. Christiāna _____
4. longa _____
5. magna _____
6. opulenta _____
8. pulchra _____
9. Rōmāna _____
10. splendida _____

D. BEING VERBS REVIEW (Give English translation of each.)
1. est _____
2. sunt _____

E. INTRANSITIVE VERBS REVIEW (Give English translation of each.)
1. ambulat _____
2. cantat _____
3. ōrat _____

F. PREPOSITION REVIEW (Give English translation of each.)
1. in _____
2. ad _____

G. CONJUNCTION REVIEW (Give English translation of each.)
1. et _____

H. ADVERB REVIEW (Give English translation of each.)
1. nōn _____

I. PREPOSITIONAL PHRASES REVIEW (Give translation of each.)
1. in villā _____
2. in casā _____
3. ad ecclēsiam _____

PART II. PRACTICAL APPLICATION

J. FORMING PLURALS (Make these first declension nouns plural.)

SINGULAR	PLURAL
1. fēmina	_____
2. puella	_____
3. villa	_____
4. ecclēsia	_____
5. via	_____
6. ancilla	_____
7. silva	_____
8. casa	_____

K. SUBJECT/VERB AGREEMENT (Circle the correct verb.)

1. Ancilla (est / sunt) bona.

2. Claudia et Octāvia (est / sunt) Rōmānæ.

3. Puella (est / sunt) pulchra.

4. Lūcia (est / sunt) Christiāna.

5. Fēminæ nōn (est / sunt) opulentæ.

6. Villa (est / sunt) splendida.

7. Portia et Antōnia (est / sunt) Christianæ.

8. Via antīqua (est / sunt) longa.

L. VERB PRACTICE (Do the subject and verb agree?)

1. Puella est bona.   Yes _____ No _____
2. Ancillæ nōn est Rōmāna.   Yes _____ No _____
3. Portia sunt Rōmāna.   Yes _____ No _____
4. Lūcia et Octāvia sunt pulchræ.   Yes _____ No _____
5. Puella ad ecclēsiam ambulat.   Yes _____ No _____
6. Lūcia ōrat.   Yes _____ No _____
7. Fēminæ sunt Christiānæ.   Yes _____ No _____
8. Ancilla est bona.   Yes _____ No _____
9. Silva sunt magna.   Yes _____ No _____

M. SUBJECT /ADJECTIVE (Underline subjects and circle adjectives.)

1. <u>Fēmina</u> est (Christiāna.)
2. Casæ nōn sunt splendidæ.
3. Octāvia est opulenta.
4. Viæ sunt longæ.
5. Claudia est pulchra.

N. PREPOSITIONAL PHRASES (Bracket prepositional phrases and translate.)

1. [In viā] fēminæ et puellæ ambulant.   *on the road*
2. Ancilla in villā laborat.   _____
3. Lūcia ambulat ad ecclesiam.   _____
4. Puellæ in casā cantant.   _____
5. In ecclēsiā fēmina bona ōrat.   _____

O. MATCHING (Match the adjective phrases with correct translations.)

____1. ancilla bona   A. the Roman women
____2. ecclēsiæ splendidæ   B. the pretty girl
____3. puella pulchra   C. a wealthy woman
____4. fēminæ Rōmānæ   D. a good maidservant
____5. silva magna   E. small cottages
____6. casæ parvæ   F. an ancient church
____7. fēmina opulenta   G. the opulent villas
____8. viæ longæ   H. a large forest
____9. villæ opulentæ   I. splendid churches
____10. ecclēsia antīqua   J. long roads

P. SENTENCE PRACTICE (Give an English translation for each sentence.)

1. Sunt bonæ.   _____
2. Via antīqua est longa.   _____
3. Antōnia in ecclēsiā ōrat.   _____
4. Puellæ sunt in casā.   _____
5. Ecclēsia est splendida.

38

THIRD PERSON SINGULAR VERBS

(Read p. 22-23 in the reader.)

- **THIRD PERSON SINGULAR VERBS** in **present** tense end in -**t**. The -**t** indicates that the subject of the verb is one person.

Fēmina ōrat.

> **Third person** means the subject is being spoken about.

> **Singular** means the subject is one person, place or thing and is represented by the pronouns he, she or it.

> **Present tense** means the action is happening now.

- **SUBJECT-VERB AGREEMENT** means that if a sentence has a **singular** subject, a verb with a **singular** ending must be used:

<u>**Familia**</u> **ōra<u>t</u>.** *The family prays.*
<u>**Aquila**</u> **vola<u>t</u>.** *The eagle flies.*
<u>**Ancilla**</u> **labora<u>t</u>.** *The maid servant works.*

Aquila magna volat.

✏ NEW **INTRANSITIVE SINGULAR VERBS** (Write each.)
   saltat *he, she, it dances*   _____
   volat *he, she, it flies*   _____

✏ NEW **FEMININE NOUNS AND ADJECTIVES** (Write each.)
   aquila, -æ, f. *eagle*   _____
   familia, -æ, f. *family*   _____
   nova *new*   _____
   recta *straight*   _____

✏️ **A. SUBJECT-VERB AGREEMENT** (Choose an appropriate singular subject for each of these sentences and write it on the line.)

1. _____ ōrat.   a. Fēmina   b. Fēminæ
2. _____ ambulat.   a. Familiæ   b. Familia
3. _____ cantat.   a. Puellæ   b. Puella
4. _____ volat.   a. Aquila   b. Aquilæ
5. _____ saltat.   a. Puellæ   b. Puella

✏️ **B. LATIN PRACTICE** (Translate each sentence.)

1. Familia est Christiāna. _____
2. Puella Rōmāna ambulat. _____
3. Ōrat. _____
4. In casā fēmina cantat. _____
5. Octāvia ambulat ad villam. _____
6. Ecclēsia est Christiāna. _____
7. Lūcia et Maria sunt bonæ. _____
8. Puella saltat. _____
9. Aquila magna volat. _____
10. Viæ sunt antīquæ. _____

✏️ **C. PRACTICE WITH PLURALS** (Give plural of each phrase and translate.)

1. puella bona   *puellae bonae (good girls)*
2. familia Christiāna _____
3. ecclēsia nova   _____
4. via longa   _____
5. via recta   _____
6. aquila magna   _____
7. villa splendida   _____
8. casa parva   _____

40

D. ENGLISH-TO-LATIN (Give the Latin equivalent of each.)

1. Portia sings. _Portia cantat._
2. She prays. _____
3. Octavia dances. _____
4. The woman walks. _____
5. The girl sings. _____
6. An eagle flies. _____
7. She sings. _____
8. Antonia walks. _____
9. The family prays. _____
10. She dances. _____

E. PREPOSITIONAL PHRASE PRACTICE (Place brackets around the prepositional phrase in each sentence.)

1. [In ecclēsiā] Portia ōrat.
2. In viā Antōnia ambulat.
3. Ancilla ad ecclēsiam ambulat.
4. Octāvia in villā ōrat.
5. Familia in viā ambulat.
6. In casā Lūcia saltat.
7. Maria in ecclēsiā ōrat.
8. In silvā aquila volat.

F. MISSING SUBJECTS (Fill in the blank with a simple or compound subject which agrees with the verb.)

1. Ad villam _____ ambulat.
2. In silvā _____ volat.
3. _____ et _____ sunt in ecclēsiā.
4. In viā _____ ambulat.
5. _____ sunt bonæ.
6. _____ ad ecclēsiam ambulat.
7. _____ et _____ sunt fēminæ Rōmānæ.
8. _____ est splendida.
9. In villā _____ saltat.
10. _____ cantat.

41

✎ **G. Missing Verbs** (Fill in the blank with an intransitive verb or being verb which agrees with the underlined subject.)

1. <u>Antōnia</u> _____.
2. <u>Aquila</u> _____.
3. <u>Lūcia et Portia</u> _____ puellae Christiānæ.
4. Ad ecclēsiam <u>familia</u> _____.
5. <u>Ancilla</u> _____ bona.
6. <u>Ecclēsiæ</u> _____ splendidæ.
7. In ecclēsiā <u>Maria</u> _____.
8. Ad villam <u>puella</u> _____.
9. In villā <u>Lūcia</u> _____.
10. <u>Casa</u> nōn _____ magna.

✎ **H. Identify Sentence Elements** (Circle the word which describes how each underlined word is being used in the sentence. Sentence elements are listed below.)

1. <u>In villā</u> Lūcia cantat. _prepositional phrase_
2. <u>Saltat</u>. _____
3. <u>Maria et Portia</u> sunt ancillae. _____
4. Via <u>est</u> recta. _____
5. Ecclēsia est <u>nova</u>. _____
6. <u>Aquila</u> est magna. _____
7. <u>Nōn</u> est opulenta. _____
8. Claudia <u>et</u> Octāvia sunt puellæ. _____

conjunction	being verb	adverb	predicate adjective
~~prepositional phrase~~	intransitive verb	subject	compound subject

42

Lesson Ten
THIRD PERSON PLURAL VERBS
(Read p. 24-27 in reader.)

• **THIRD PERSON SINGULAR VERBS** In the last lesson we learned about third person singular verbs with the ending **-t.** Now we will learn about third person plural verbs. Notice the **-nt** ending:

Fēminæ ōrant.

Third person means the subject is being spoken about.

Present tense means the action is happening now.

Plural means the subject is more than one person, place or thing and is represented by the pronoun they.

✎ **NEW INTRANSITIVE PLURAL VERBS** (Write each.)
habitant *they live*   _____
stant *they stand*   _____
ambulant *they walk*   _____
laborant *they work*   _____

• **SUBJECT-VERB AGREEMENT WITH PLURAL VERBS** means that if a sentence has a **plural** subject, a verb with a **plural** ending must be used.

In villā puellæ habitant. *The girls live in a villa.*
Aquilæ volant. *Eagles fly.*

Altæ columnæ stant.

✎ **NEW ADJECTIVES TO LEARN** (Write each.)
alta* *tall*   _____
glōriōsa *glorious*   _____

* The adjective **alta** is an *adjective of quantity* since it denotes length, so it will come *before* the noun it modifies: **alta columna**, a tall column.

✎ **A. LATIN NOUN PRACTICE** (Write the plural of each noun.)
1. āra, -æ, f. *altar*   *arae*
2. columna, -æ, f. *column*   _____
3. fenestra, -æ, f. *window*   _____
4. statua, -æ, f. *statue*   _____

✎ **B. GRAMMAR QUESTIONS** (Circle the word that completes the sentence.)
1. If there is a **plural** subject, the verb must be **(singular / plural)**.
2. **Third person (singular / plural)** verbs end in **-nt**.
3. **"Third person"** means the **(subject / verb)** is being spoken about.
4. **Present tense** means the action is happening **(now / in the future.)**
5. **Sunt** is a **(singular / plural)** being verb.
6. **Est** is a **(singular / plural)** being verb.

✎ **C. ADJECTIVE PHRASES** (Is the adjective phrase singular or plural?)
1. **alta columna**   singular   plural
2. **statua pulchra**   singular   plural
3. **altæ columnæ**   singular   plural
4. **fenestræ glōriōsæ**   singular   plural
5. **ecclēsia antīqua**   singular   plural
6. **āra splendida**   singular   plural
7. **fenestra glōriōsa**   singular   plural
8. **statuæ pulchræ**   singular   plural
9. **ecclēsiæ antīquæ**   singular   plural
10. **āræ splendidæ**   singular   plural

✎ **D. SUBJECT-VERB AGREEMENT** (Which verb agrees with the subject?)
1. <u>Puella</u> _____ in ecclēsia.   a. ōrat   b. ōrant
2. <u>Lūcia et Portia</u> _____ Rōmānæ.   a. est   b. sunt
3. <u>Ancillæ</u> _____ in villā.   a. laborat   b. laborant
4. <u>Familiæ</u> ad ecclēsiam _____.   a. ambulat   b. ambulant
5. <u>Via</u> _____ antīqua.   a. est   b. sunt
6. In silvā <u>aquila</u> _____.   a. volat   b. volant
7. In casā <u>fēmina</u> _____.   a. habitat   b. habitant
8. Alta <u>columna</u> _____.   a. stat   b. stant

44

E. Matching (Find the best verb for each sentence.)

____ 1. Fēminæ in viā _____.
____ 2. In villā ancilla _____.
____ 3. In ecclēsia familiæ _____.
____ 4. Statuæ _____.
____ 5. Ancillæ bonæ _____.
____ 6. In villā Octāvia et Claudia _____.
____ 7. Alta columna _____.
____ 8. Aquilæ _____.
____ 9. In casā Portia _____.
____ 10. In silvā aquila _____.

A. volat
B. laborant
C. cantat
D. ambulant
E. ōrant
F. habitant
G. stant
H. volant
I. laborat
J. stat

F. Latin-to-English (Give the English equivalent of these Latin verbs.)

1. Stat. _____*he, she, it stands*_____
2. Ōrat. _____
3. Habitant. _____
4. Cantat. _____
5. Ambulat. _____
6. Saltant. _____
7. Volat. _____
8. Cantant. _____
9. Laborat. _____
10. Habitat. _____
11. Cantant. _____
12. Laborant. _____
13. Stant. _____
14. Saltat. _____
15. Ambulant. _____

G. Sentence Elements Practice (Underline subjects, circle adjectives, bracket the prepositional phrases and draw two lines under the verbs.)

1. Puella Christiāna [ad ecclēsiam] ambulat.
2. Fenestræ glōriōsæ sunt in ecclēsiā.
3. In villā ancilla bona laborat.
4. Āra splendida in ecclēsiā stat.
5. In silvā aquilæ magnæ volant.

✎ **H. MISSING MACRONS** (Place the macrons where needed in these adjective phrases and translate each.)

1. **ara gloriosa** _____ *a glorious altar* _____
2. **fenestra gloriosa** _____
3. **ecclesia nova** _____
4. **ara splendida** _____
5. **via Romana** _____
6. **ecclesia antiqua** _____
7. **femina Christiana** _____
8. **casa Romana** _____
9. **silva antiqua** _____
10. **puella Romana** _____

✎ **I. MISSING ADJECTIVES** (Refer to the phrases above and fill in the blanks with adjectives which describe the underlined subjects and agree in number.)

1. <u>**Aquilæ**</u> _____ **volant.**

2. <u>**Fenestræ**</u> _____ **sunt in ecclēsiā.**

3. **Ad villam** <u>**fēminæ**</u> _____ **ambulant.**

4. **Ancilla** _____ **laborat.**

5. **In villā familia** _____ **habitat.**

6. **Fēmina** _____ **ad ecclēsiam ambulat.**

7. _____ **columnæ in villā stant.**

8. **Puella** _____ **cantat.**

✎ **J. ADJECTIVE PHRASE PRACTICE** (Create appropriate adjective phrase for each image.)

_____   _____   _____   _____

46

LESSON ELEVEN
PREDICATE NOMINATIVES AND PREDICATE ADJECTIVES
(Read p. 28-29 in the reader.)

• **PREDICATE NOMINATIVES** are **nouns** or **pronouns** which follow a being verb and rename or describe the subject.

Italia

Ītalia est pæninsula.

subject   being verb   predicate nominative

• **PREDICATE ADJECTIVES** are **adjectives** which follow a being verb and describe or give more information about the **subject**.

Fēminæ sunt bonæ.

subject   being verb   predicate adjective

Predicate nominatives and **predicate adjectives** must agree with the subjects they modify. If a subject is **plural**, the predicate nominative or predicate adjective must also be **plural**.

Mons Ætna est nōta.

✏ **NEW ADJECTIVES TO LEARN** (Write on line.)
nōta *famous* (**noh**/tah) _____

✏ **NEW LATIN NOUNS PRACTICE** (Write each.)
insula, -æ, f. *island* _____
Ītalia, -æ, f. *Italy* _____
Mons Ætna, f. *Mount Aetna* _____
pæninsula, -æ, f. *peninsula* _____
Sicilia, -æ, f. *Sicily*

• **NEW PREPOSITION *PROPE*** is translated as *near, next to*. First declension singular nouns used with the preposition **ad** end in **-am**.

prope Ītaliam *near Italy*

A. PREDICATE NOMINATIVES OR ADJECTIVES? (Is the underlined word a predicate nominative or a predicate adjective?)

1. **Maria est fēmina.** (predicate nominative)   predicate adjective
2. **Ītālia est pæninsula.**   predicate nominative   predicate adjective
3. **Fēminæ sunt Rōmānæ.**   predicate nominative   predicate adjective
4. **Sicilia est insula.**   predicate nominative   predicate adjective
5. **Insulæ sunt parvæ.**   predicate nominative   predicate adjective

B. PREDICATE NOMINATIVES (Choose an appropriate noun.)

   insula   puella   pæninsula   fēmina   ancilla

1. **Lūcia est** _____.
2. **Ītalia nōn est** _____.
3. **Octāvia est** _____.
4. **Ītalia est** _____.
5. **Sicilia est** _____.

C. PREDICATE ADJECTIVES (Choose an appropriate adjective.)

   parva   nōta   magna   antīqua   Christiāna   longa

1. **Mons Ætna est** _____.
2. **Ecclēsia est** _____.
3. **Via est** _____.
4. **Pæninsula nōn est** _____.
5. **Puella est** _____.

D. PREPOSITIONAL PHRASE PRACTICE (Match the translations.)

_____1. prope insulam   A. near the forest
_____2. prope Ītaliam   B. near the island
_____3. prope silvam   C. near the cottage
_____4. prope casam   D. near the peninsula
_____5. prope Siciliam   E. near Italy
_____6. prope pæninsulam   F. near Sicily

✏️ **E. MORE PREPOSITIONAL PHRASES** (Place brackets around the prepositional phrase in each sentence.)

1. [Ad ecclēsiam] puallæ ambulant.
2. Prope silvam Lūcia ambulat.
3. Maria et Portia ad ecclēsiam ambulant.
4. Antōnia in villā habitat.
5. Familiæ in viā ambulant.
6. In casā puellæ saltant.
7. Sicilia est prope Ītaliam.
8. Aquilæ prope silvam volant.
9. Pæninsula est prope insulam.
10. In ecclesiā altæ columnæ stant.

✏️ **F. MISSING PREDICATE ADJECTIVES** (Fill in the blanks with the predicate adjective which agrees in number with the underlined subject.)

1. <u>Insulæ</u> sunt _____.   nōta   nōtæ
2. <u>Fenestræ</u> sunt _____.   splendida   splendidæ
3. <u>Aquila</u> est _____.   magna   magnæ
4. <u>Ancillæ</u> nōn sunt _____.   Rōmāna   Rōmānæ
5. <u>Via</u> nōn est _____.   recta   rectæ
6. <u>Silva</u> est _____.   antīqua   antīquæ
7. <u>Columnæ</u> sunt _____.   alta   altæ
8. <u>Āra</u> est _____.   glōriōsa   glōriōsæ

✏️ **G. MISSING PREDICATE NOMINATIVES** (Fill in the blanks with the predicate nominative which agrees in number with the underlined subject.)

1. <u>Sicilia</u> est _____.   insula   insulæ
2. <u>Maria et Portia</u> sunt _____.   ancilla   ancillæ
3. <u>Antōnia</u> est _____.   fēmina   fēminæ
4. <u>Claudia</u> nōn est _____.   ancilla   ancillæ
5. <u>Ītalia</u> nōn est _____.   insula   insulæ
6. <u>Octāvia et Claudia</u> sunt _____.   puella   puellæ

49

✎ **H. LATIN-TO-ENGLISH** (Give a Latin translation for these simple sentences. Sentences without a definitive subject may use *he, she, it* or *they*.)

1. Prope silvam aquila volat.

_____

2. Ecclēsiæ Christiānæ sunt splendidæ.

_____

3. In ecclēsia sunt fenestræ glōriōsæ.

_____

4. Viæ in Siciliā nōn sunt longæ.

_____

5. Viæ Rōmānæ sunt rectæ.

_____

6. Sicilia est insula nōta.

_____

7. Sicilia est insula magna in Eurōpā.

_____

8. In villā altæ columnæ stant.

_____

✎ **I. SENTENCE ELEMENTS PRACTICE** (Identify the underlined word in each sentence as a **subject, being verb, intransitive verb, adjective, predicate adjective, predicate nominative, adverb, conjunction** or **prepositional phrase.**)

1. Ad ecclēsiam puellæ <u>ambulant</u>. *intransitive verb*

2. <u>Mons Ætna</u> est nōta. _____

3. Ancilla <u>bona</u> laborat. _____

4. Āra splendida <u>in ecclēsiā</u> stat. _____

5. Via Rōmāna est <u>recta</u>. _____

6. Sicilia est <u>insula</u>. _____

7. Maria <u>nōn</u> est Rōmāna. _____

8. Lūcia <u>et</u> Portia sunt Christiānae. _____

9. Ītalia <u>est</u> pæninsula. _____

MORE ADJECTIVE PHRASES
(Read p. 30-31 in the reader.)

•**ADJECTIVE PHRASES:** In the reader you will find longer sentences with **adjective phrases.** In the sentence below, there is an adjective phrase which describes the subject:

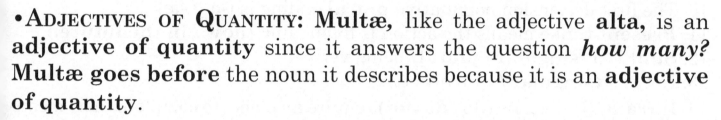

Claudia est f̄emina R̄om̄ana.

subject   being verb   adjective

predicate nominative

•**ADJECTIVES OF QUANTITY: Mult̄æ,** like the adjective **alta,** is an **adjective of quantity** since it answers the question *how many?* **Mult̄æ goes before** the noun it describes because it is an **adjective of quantity.**

mult̄æ insul̄æ *many islands*
mult̄æ eccl̄esīæ *many churches*

▶*Adjectives of quantity usually go before the nouns they modify.*

✎ **NEW LATIN NOUNS PRACTICE** (Write each.)
terra, -æ, f. *land, country* _____

✎ **A. ADJECTIVE PHRASE PRACTICE** (Underline adjective phrases.)
1. **Oct̄avia est <u>puella bona</u>.**
2. **Luc̄ia est f̄emina opulenta.**
3. **̄Italia est pæninsula magna.**
4. **In ̄Italīa eccl̄esīæ splendid̄æ sunt.**
5. **F̄emin̄æ R̄om̄an̄æ in vīa ambulant.**
6. **Fenestr̄æ gl̄orīos̄æ in eccl̄esīa sunt.**
7. **In eccl̄esīa ̄ara splendida est.**
8. **Insul̄æ parv̄æ prope ̄Italiam sunt.**
9. **̄Italia est pæninsula n̄ota.**
10. **Sicilia est insula magna.**

51

✎ B. GRAMMAR QUESTIONS (Circle the word which completes the sentence.)

1. Adjectives of **quantity** usually go (**before / after**) the nouns they describe.
2. Adjectives of **quality** usually go (**before / after**) the nouns they describe.
3. **Third person (singular / plural)** verbs in **present** tense end in -t.
4. **Third person (singular / plural)** verbs in **present** tense end in **-nt**.
5. "**Third person**" means the (**subject / verb**) is being spoken about.
6. **Predicate nominatives** are (**nouns / adjectives**) which follow a being verb and rename or describe the **subject**.
7. **Predicate adjectives** are (**nouns / adjectives**) which follow a being verb and rename or describe the **subject**.
8. If there is a **plural** subject, the verb must be (**singular / plural**).
9. The first declension nominative **singular** ending is (-a / -æ).
10. The first declension nominative **plural** ending is (-a / -æ).
11. **Present tense** means the action is happening (**now / in the future.**)
12. **Sunt** is a (**singular / plural**) being verb.
13. **Est** is a (**singular / plural**) being verb.
14. **Intransitive verbs (do / do not)** require an object to complete their meaning in a sentence.
15. **Ōrat, cantat** and **ambulat** are (**intransitive / being**) verbs.

✎ C. SUBJECT-VERB AGREEMENT (Choose the verb which agrees with the underlined <u>subject</u> in each sentence.)

1. <u>Fēminæ</u> _____ in ecclēsiā.   a. ōrat   b. ōrant
2. <u>Claudia</u> _____ Rōmāna.   a. est   b. sunt
3. <u>Familia</u> _____ in casā.   a. habitat   b. habitant
4. <u>Ancillæ</u> in villā _____.   a. laborat   b. laborant
5. <u>Aquila</u> _____.   a. volat   b. volant
6. <u>Columnæ</u> in ecclēsiā _____.   a. stat   b. stant
7. <u>Puellæ</u> in silvā _____.   a. saltat   b. saltant
8. <u>Sicilia</u> prope Ītaliam _____.   a. est   b. sunt
9. <u>Āra</u> in ecclēsiā _____.   a. stat   b. stant
10. <u>Casæ</u> _____ prope silvam.   a. est   b. sunt
11. <u>Octāvia</u> _____.   a. cantat   b. cantant
12. <u>Ītalia</u> **nōn** _____ insula.   a. est   b. sunt

✎ **D. IDENTIFICATION** (Underline the **subjects** in these sentences.)
1. Fenestræ sunt glōriōsæ.
2. Octāvia est puella bona.
3. Ītalia est pæninsula.
4. Insulæ sunt magnæ.
5. Terra est antīqua.
6. Ītalia est terra Christiāna.
7. Statuæ sunt pulchræ.
8. Multæ insulæ sunt nōtæ.
9. Via est nova.
10. Aquilæ sunt magnæ.

✎ **E. SUBJECT / VERB AGREEMENT** (Circle the being verb which agrees with the underlined subject in each of these sentences.)
1. <u>Puella</u> (est / sunt) Rōmāna.
2. <u>Fēminæ</u> (est / sunt) bonæ.
3. <u>Claudia et Octāvia</u> nōn (est / sunt) Christiānæ.
4. <u>Familiæ</u> (est / sunt) opulentæ.
5. <u>Fenestra</u> (est / sunt) nova.
6. <u>Statua</u> (est / sunt) antīqua.
7. <u>Ītalia</u> (est / sunt) terra nōta.
8. <u>Viæ</u> nōn (est / sunt) rectæ.
9. <u>Pertia et Maria</u> (est / sunt) ancillæ.
10. <u>Insula</u> (est / sunt) prope Ītaliam.

✎ **F. IDENTIFICATION** (Underline each verb. Is it singular or plural?)

1. In Ītaliā familia habitat.	singular	plural
2. Fēminæ in ecclēsiā ōrant.	singular	plural
3. Maria et Lūcia ambulant.	singular	plural
4. Claudia cantat.	singular	plural
5. In villā ancillæ laborant.	singular	plural

✎ **G. IDENTIFICATION** (Underline each **adjective phrase** and translate.)

1. <u>Multæ ecclēsiæ</u> sunt in Ītaliā. _many churches_
2. Antōnia nōn est fēmina opulenta. _____
3. Ītalia est pæninsula longa. _____
4. Sicilia est insula nōta. _____
5. Sunt puellæ Rōmānæ. _____
6. Multæ aquilæ in silvā volant. _____
7. Est terra antīqua. _____
8. Nōn sunt viæ longæ in Siciliā. _____
9. Sicilia est insula nōta. _____
10. Octāvia est puella Rōmāna. _____

✎ **H. ENGLISH-TO-LATIN** (Give Latin translation of these adjective phrases.)

1. many islands _____
2. many lands _____
3. many peninsulas _____
4. many eagles _____
5. many columns _____
6. many windows _____
7. many girls _____
8. many women _____
9. many churches _____
10. many roads _____

✎ **I. MISSING MACRONS** (Place the macrons on the long vowels in these adjective phrases and translate each.)

1. terra antiqua _____
2. insula nota _____
3. via Romana _____
4. pæninsula nota _____
5. multæ ecclesiæ _____
6. statua gloriosa _____
7. familia Christiana _____
8. ecclesia antiqua _____

LESSONS 9-12 REVIEW

PART I. CONCEPT AND VOCABULARY REVIEW

A. GRAMMAR REVIEW (Circle the correct word in the parentheses.)

1. (Singular / Plural) nouns refer to more than one person, place or thing.
2. (Singular / Plural) nouns refer to one person, place or thing.
3. An (adjective / adverb) is a word which describes a noun or pronoun.
4. Est is a (singular / plural) being verb.
5. Sunt is a (singular / plural) being verb.
6. (Nouns / Prepositions) are words that name persons, places or things.
7. The first declension nominative singular ending is (-a / -æ).
8. The first declension nominative plural ending is (-a / -æ).
9. Latin nouns are placed in groups called (declensions / conjugations).
10. Most first declension nouns are (feminine / masculine.)
11. The (subject / preposition) is the person, place or thing the sentence is about.
12. (In / Ad) may be translated as *in, on* or *upon.*
13. Nōn is an (adverb / adjective).
14. Et is a (conjunction / preposition) which joins words together.
15. In is a (conjunction / preposition) showing relationship between words.
16. In silvā is a (conjunction / prepositional phrase.)
17. Adjectives of quality are usually placed (before / after) nouns they modify.
18. Latin adjectives (must / must not) agree with the nouns they modify in case, number and gender.
19. Intransitive verbs (do / do not) require an object to complete their meaning.
20. Ōrat, cantat and ambulat are (intransitive / being) verbs.
21. Third person (singular / plural) verbs end in -nt.
22. Present tense means the action is happening (now / in the future.)
23. Predicate (nominatives / adjectives) are nouns or pronouns which follow a being verb and rename or describe the subject.
24. Predicate (nominatives /adjectives) are adjectives which follow a being verb and rename or describe the subject.
25. "Third person" means the (subject / verb) is being spoken about.

B. FIRST DECLENSION NOUN REVIEW (Translate and give the gender of each.)

#	Noun	Translation		
1.	ancilla	_____	feminine	masculine
2.	aquila	_____	feminine	masculine
3.	āra	_____	feminine	masculine
4.	casa	_____	feminine	masculine
5.	columna	_____	feminine	masculine
6.	ecclēsia	_____	feminine	masculine
7.	familia	_____	feminine	masculine
8.	fēmina	_____	feminine	masculine
9.	fenestra	_____	feminine	masculine
10.	insula	_____	feminine	masculine
11.	Ītalia	_____	feminine	masculine
12.	Mons Ætna	_____	feminine	masculine
13.	pæninsula	_____	feminine	masculine
14.	puella	_____	feminine	masculine
15.	Sicilia	_____	feminine	masculine
16.	silva	_____	feminine	masculine
17.	statua	_____	feminine	masculine
18.	terra	_____	feminine	masculine
19.	via	_____	feminine	masculine
20.	villa	_____	feminine	masculine

C. FIRST DECLENSION ADJECTIVE REVIEW (Define each.)

1. alta _____
2. antīqua _____
3. bona _____
4. Christiāna _____
5. glōriōsa _____
6. longa _____
7. magna _____
8. Multæ _____
9. nova _____
10. opulenta _____
11. parva _____
12. pulchra _____
13. recta _____
14. Rōmāna _____
15. splendida _____

D. INTRANSITIVE VERBS REVIEW (Define and give the number of each.)

1. ambulat _____ singular plural
2. ambulant _____ singular plural
3. cantat _____ singular plural
4. cantant _____ singular plural
5. habitat _____ singular plural
6. habitant _____ singular plural
7. laborat _____ singular plural
8. laborant _____ singular plural
9. ōrat _____ singular plural
10. ōrant _____ singular plural
11. saltat _____ singular plural
12. saltant _____ singular plural
13. stat _____ singular plural
14. stant _____ singular plural
15. volat _____ singular plural
16. volant _____ singular plural

E. BEING VERB REVIEW (Define and give the number of each.)

1. est _____ singular plural
2. sunt _____ singular plural

F. PREPOSITION REVIEW (Define.)

1. in _____
2. ad _____
3. prope _____

G. CONJUNCTION REVIEW (Define.)

1. et _____

H. ADVERB REVIEW (Define.)

1. nōn _____

I. PREPOSITIONAL PHRASES REVIEW (Translate each.)

1. in villā _____
2. in casā _____
3. ad ecclēsiam _____
4. prope insulam _____

57

Part II. Practical Application

J. Forming Nominative Plurals (Make these nouns plural.)
1. terra   _____
2. fenestra   _____
3. columna   _____
4. via   _____
5. insula   _____

K. Subjects and Verbs (Do the subject and verb agree?)
1. <u>Aquilae</u> volant.   Yes ____ No ____
2. <u>Fēmina</u> ambulat.   Yes ____ No ____
3. <u>Maria et Lūcia</u> laborant.   Yes ____ No ____
4. <u>Via</u> est recta.   Yes ____ No ____
5. <u>Puellæ</u> saltant.   Yes ____ No ____

L. Subject/Verb Agreement (Which verb agrees with the subject?)
1. Āra splendida (stat / stant) in ecclēsiā.
2. Fenestra (est / sunt) glōriōsa.
3. In villā familia (habitat /habitant).
4. In silvā aquila (volat / volant).
5. Columnæ (est / sunt) altæ.

M. Predicate Nominative /Adjective Identification (Is the underlined word a predicate nominative or a predicate adjective?)

1. Ītalia est <u>pæninsula</u>.   predicate nominative   predicate adjective
2. Aquila est <u>magna</u>.   predicate nominative   predicate adjective
3. Vīllæ sunt <u>opulēntæ</u>.   predicate nominative   predicate adjective
4. Portia est <u>ancilla</u>.   predicate nominative   predicate adjective
5. Mons Ætna est <u>nōta</u>.   predicate nominative   predicate adjective

N. PREPOSITIONAL PHRASE IDENTIFICATION (Place brackets around each prepositional phrase and write on line.)

1. [In casā parvā] puella habitat. ___*in a small cottage*___

2. In ecclēsiā altæ columnæ stant. _____

3. Aquila volat prope silvam. _____

4. Ad villam ambulat. _____

5. In viā longā ancillæ ambulant. _____

O. MATCHING (Match the adjective phrases with correct English translations.)

____1. āra splendida   A. the large eagles

____2. fenestræ glōriōsæ   B. glorious windows

____3. Multæ īnsulæ   C. a good maidservant

____4. terra antīqua   D. the famous peninsula

____5. silva magna   E. the splendid altar

____6. viæ novæ   F. beautiful statues

____7. via recta   G. many islands

____8. villæ opulēntæ   H. a long island

____9. puella Rōmāna   I. straight road

____10. aquilæ magnæ   J. Roman girl

____11. insula longa   K. an ancient land

____12. pæninsula nōta   L. the ancient church

____13. statuæ pūlchræ   M. a great forest

____14. ancilla bona   N. opulent villas

____15. ecclēsia antīqua   O. new roads

P. SENTENCE TRANSLATION (Translate each sentence.)

1. Cantant et saltant.

_____

2. Viæ in Siciliā nōn sunt longæ.

_____

3. Ītalia est terra antīqua.

_____

4. Silvæ sunt magnæ.

_____

5. Familia in pæninsulā habitat.

_____

Q. SUBJECT IDENTIFICATION (Draw a line under the subject in each sentence.)
1. Puella in viā ambulat. _____
2. Viā nōn est rectā. _____
3. Aquilæ volant. _____
4. Ītalia est pæninsula. _____
5. Sicilia est insula. _____
6. Ancillæ nōn sunt Rōmānæ. _____
7. Maria et Lūcia cantant. _____
8. Ad ecclēsiam Lūcia ambulat. _____
9. Āra est splendida. _____
10. Aquila volat. _____

R. INTRANSITIVE VERBS (Underline the verb. Is it singular or plural?)
1. Ancilla in casā lāborat.   singular   plural
2. In silvā aquilæ volant.   singular   plural
3. Lūcia cantat.   singular   plural
4. Columna stat.   singular   plural
5. Famīliæ in ecclēsiā orant.   singular   plural

S. PROOFREADING (Draw a line each spelling mistakes and write corrected word.)
1. ~~Fæmina~~ ambulat. _femina_
2. Prope casam aqīla volat. _____
3. Ītaliat est terra antīqua. _____
4. Alta colōmna stat in ecclēsiā. _____
5. Sunt Multæ eclēsiæ in Ītalia. _____
6. Vīllæ eunt splendidæ. _____
7. Ad ecclēsiam āimbulat. _____
8. Via est rōcta. _____
9. Sicilia est insula māna. _____
10. Pullæ sunt Rōmānæ. _____

MORE PREPOSITIONAL PHRASES
(Read p. 32-33 in the reader.)

• **THE PREPOSITION *IN*** is translated as *in, on,* or *upon* as the context requires. The preposition **in** is usally followed by a noun object in the **ablative case**. The noun object can be singular or plural.

The singular ending for the noun object of the preposition in the first declension ablative case is **-a**, and the plural ending is **-is.**

in silvā *in the forest*   **in villā** *in the villa*   **in casā** *in the cottage*
in silvīs *in the forests*   **in villīs** *in the villas*   **in casīs** *in cottages*

The noun object of the preposition **in** may sometimes be modified by adjectives which must agree with the noun in **case, number and gender**. In the following examples the noun objects are modified by adjectives which share the same **case** (ablative), **gender** (feminine), and **number** (singular or plural). Note that an adjective of quality usually follows the noun it modifies.

in casā parvā *in the small house*

preposition   noun object of preposition   adjective

in silvā densā *in the dense forest*
in silvīs densīs *in the dense forests*

in casā parvā *in the small cottage*
in casīs pārvīs *in small cottages*

In casā parvā habitant.

• **THE PREPOSITION SUPER** is translated as ***over, above.*** First declension **singular** nouns used with the preposition *super* end in **-am.** First declension **plural** nouns used with *super* end in **-ās.**

super silvam *over the forest*
super silvās *over the forests*

✏️ **A. GRAMMAR QUESTIONS** (Circle the word which completes the sentence.)
1. Adjectives of **quantity** usually go (**before / after**) the nouns they describe.
2. Adjectives of **quality** usually go (**before / after**) the nouns they describe.
3. **Third person (singular / plural)** verbs in **present** tense end in **-t**.
4. **Third person (singular / plural)** verbs in **present** tense end in **-nt**.
5. "**Third person**" means the (**subject / verb**) is being spoken about.
6. **Predicate (nominatives / adjectives)** are **nouns** or **pronouns** which follow a being verb and rename or describe the **subject**.
7. **Predicate (nominatives / adjectives)** are **adjectives** which follow a being verb and rename or describe the **subject**.

✏️ **B. ADJECTIVE PHRASES** (Match each phrase with its translation.)

_____1. **pæninsula nōta**	**A. many lands**
_____2. **fēminæ Christiānæ**	**B. ancient lands**
_____3. **ecclēsiæ splendidæ**	**C. Christian family**
_____4. **fenestra glōriōsa**	**D. good girl**
_____5. **casa parva**	**E. ancient church**
_____6. **mūltae insulæ**	**F. Christian women**
_____7. **statua pulchra**	**G. long roads**
_____8. **terræ antīquæ**	**H. glorious window**
_____9. **puella bona**	**I. famous peninsula**
_____10. **ecclēsia antīqua**	**J. many islands**
_____11. **multæ terræ**	**K. wealthy villa**
_____12. **familia Christiāna**	**L. beautiful statue**
_____13. **villa opulenta**	**M. small forest**
_____14. **silva parva**	**N. splendid churches**
_____15. **viæ longæ**	**O. small cottage**

✏️ **C. PREDICATE NOMINATIVES OR ADJECTIVES?** (Is the underlined word a predicate nominative or a predicate adjective?)
1. **Āra est <u>magna</u>.**   predicate nominative   predicate adjective
2. **Ītalia est <u>pæninsula</u>.** predicate nominative   predicate adjective
3. **Mons Ætna est <u>nōta</u>.** predicate nominative   predicate adjective
4. **Sicilia est <u>insula</u>.**   predicate nominative   predicate adjective
5. **Silva sunt <u>antīqua</u>.** predicate nominative   predicate adjective

✎ **D. Missing Prepositional Phrases** (Fill in the blank with the correct Latin prepositional phrase from the choices below.)

1. Puellæ *(to the church)* ambulant. _____*ad ecclesiam*_____
2. *(In the villa)* ancilla lāborat. _____
3. *(Near the forest)* aquilæ volant. _____
4. *(Over the forest)* aquila volat. _____
5. Insula est *(near Italy)*. _____
6. *(In the cottage)* familia habitat. _____
7. *(To the villa)* ancillæ ambulant. _____
8. *(Near the cottage)* Lūcia saltat. _____
9. *(In the church)* fēminæ ōrant. _____

prope silvam	prope casam	prope Ītaliam
in ecclēsiā	in villā	in casā
super silvam	ad villam	~~ad ecclēsiam~~

✎ **E. Prepositional Phrases** (Match each phrase with its translation.)

_____1. in the forests   A. in ecclēsiā antīquā
_____2. on the long road   B. super silvās
_____3. in the cottages   C. in Ītaliā
_____4. over the forests   D. ad insulam
_____5. near the church   E. prope pæninsulam
_____6. in the ancient church   F. super silvam
_____7. in the small cottage   G. ad ecclēsiās
_____8. on the straight road   H. prope silvam
_____9. over the forest   I. prope āram splendidam
_____10. in Italy   J. prope ecclēsiam
_____11, near the peninsula   K. in viā rectā
_____12. to the island   L. in casīs
_____13. to the churches   M. in silvīs
_____14. near the forest   N. in casā parvā
_____15. near the splendid altar O. in viā longā

✏️ **F. Sentence Elements Practice** (Identify the underline word in each sentence as a **subject, being verb, intransitive verb, adjective, predicate adjective, predicate nominative, adverb, conjunction, preposition** or **object of a preposition**.)

1. Puella <u>in</u> viā ambulat. _____preposition_____
2. Via <u>nōn</u> est rectā. _____
3. Prope silvam aquilæ <u>volant</u>. _____
4. Ītalia est <u>pæninsula</u>. _____
5. <u>Sicilia</u> est insula. _____
6. Ancillæ nōn <u>sunt</u> Rōmānæ. _____
7. In viā Maria <u>et</u> Lūcia ambulant. _____
8. Ad <u>ecclēsiam</u> Lūcia ambulat. _____
9. Āra est <u>splendida</u>. _____
10. Aquila <u>magna</u> volat. _____

✏️ **G. Missing Subjects** (Supply a first declension noun as the missing subject in each sentence, making sure it agrees with the verb.)

1. _____ et _____ in viā ambulant.
2. _____ sunt rectæ.
3. Prope silvam _____ volat.
4. _____ est insula.
5. _____ est nōta.
6. _____ nōn est Rōmāna.
7. In viā _____ ambulat.
8. In ecclēsiā splēndidā _____ cantat.
9. _____ sunt splendidæ.
10. _____ magnæ volant.
11. _____ nōn est Christiāna.
12. In casīs _____ habitant.
13. _____ sunt pūlchræ.
14. In ecclēsiā sunt _____ glōriōsæ.
15. Altæ _____ stant prope āram.

LESSON FOURTEEN
ADJECTIVE / NOUN AGREEMENT
(Read p. 34-37 in the reader.)

• **ADJECTIVE / NOUN AGREEMENT:** An adjective must agree with the noun it modifies in **case, number,** and **gender.** This means that if, as in the example below, the noun in an adjective phrase is a **nominative singular feminine** noun, then its adjective must also have a **nominative singular feminine** ending:

columba alba *a white dove*

first declension feminine singular nominative noun

first declension feminine singular nominative adjective

The Latin adjective **alba,** *white,* is listed in the Latin dictionary in the following way:

albus, -a, -um, adj. *white*

first declension nominative **masculine** singular ending **-us**

first declension nominative **feminine** singular ending **-a**

first declension nominative **neuter** singular ending **-um**

Three endings are listed, indicating that this adjective has endings in the three genders of Latin nouns and adjectives: **masculine, feminine** and **neuter.**

First and second declension adjectives are those adjectives which use first and second declension endings to modify feminine, masculine or neuter nouns and will usually be listed in the Latin dictionary with the endings **-us, -a, -um.** In the following example, a **nominative** (case) **plural** (number) **feminine** (gender) noun modified by an adjective with a **nominative plural feminine** ending:

columbæ albæ *white doves*

▶ *Adjectives agree with the nouns in case, number, and gender.*

✎ **NEW ADJECTIVES PRACTICE** (Write each.)
albus, -a, -um *white* _____
densus, -a, -um *thick, dense* _____
rubrus, -a, -um *red* _____
speciōsus, -a, -um *beautiful* _____

NEW LATIN NOUNS PRACTICE (Write each.)
rosa, -æ, f. *rose* _____

columba, -æ, f. *dove* _____

INTRANSITIVE VERB PRACTICE (Write each.)
murmurat *he, she, it murmurs* _____

murmurant *they murmur* _____

A. ADJECTIVE PHRASE PRACTICE (Make each singular phrase plural.)
1. **columba speciōsa** *columbae speciosae*
2. **familia Christiāna** _____
3. **ancilla bona** _____
4. **fenestra glōriōsa** _____
5. **āra splendida** _____
6. **alta columna** _____
7. **rosa rubra** _____
8. **casa parva** _____

B. PROOFREADING (Underline spelling errors and write correction.)
1. ~~Sont~~ rosæ rubræ prope casam. *Sunt* _____
2. Lucīa in casā parvā haebitat. _____
3. Ītalia est tēra antīqua. _____
4. Ōrat in eclēsiā splēndidā. _____
5. Sunt meltæ ecclēsiæ. _____
6. Alta collummna in ecclēsiā stat. _____

C. GRAMMAR QUESTIONS (Circle the word which completes the sentence.)
1. A subject is **singular / plural** if it is **one** person, place or thing.
2. A subject is **singular / plural** if it is **more than one** person, place or thing.
3. "**Third person**" means the (**subject / verb**) is being spoken about.
4. Adjectives of **quantity** usually go (**before / after**) the nouns they describe.
5. Adjectives of **quality** usually go (**before / after**) the nouns they describe.
6. **Third person (singular / plural)** verbs in **present** tense end in **-t.**
7. **Third person (singular / plural)** verbs in **present** tense end in **-nt.**
8. **Predicate (nominatives / adjectives)** are **nouns** or **pronouns** which follow a being verb and rename or describe the **subject.**
9. **Predicate (nominatives / adjectives)** are **adjectives** which follow a being verb and rename or describe the **subject.**

D. MISSING ADJECTIVES (Fill in the blanks with the adjective which agrees in number with the underlined noun.)

1. <u>Insula</u> _nota_ est Sicilia.   (nōta)   nōtæ
2. <u>Rosæ</u> _____ sunt prope casam.   alba   albæ
3. <u>Aquila</u> _____ in silvā volat.   magna   magnæ
4. Maria nōn est <u>puella</u> _____.   Rōmāna   Rōmānæ
5. Nōn sunt <u>viæ</u> _____.   recta   rectæ
6. <u>Silva</u> _____ est in Ītaliā.   antīqua   antīquæ
7. <u>Columba</u> _____ murmurat.   speciōsa   speciōsæ
8. _____ <u>columnæ</u> stant in ecclēsiā.   Alta   Altæ
9. <u>Famliæ</u> _____ ōrant.   Christiāna   Christiānæ
10. Est <u>fēmina</u> _____.   bona   bonæ
11. Ītalia est <u>terra</u> _____.   antīqua   antīquæ
12. Sicilia est <u>insula</u> _____.   magna   magnæ
13. <u>Puellæ</u> _____ in viā ambulant.   bona   bonæ
14. Sunt <u>fenestræ</u> _____ in villā.   glōriōsa   glōriōsæ
15. Est <u>āra</u> _____ in ecclēsiā.   splendida   splendidæ

E. PREPOSITIONAL PHRASE PRACTICE (Match the prepositional phrases in English with its Latin equivalent.)

_____1. in the cottages   A. in silvīs
_____2. over the forests   B. in viā
_____3. to the church   C. ad insulās
_____4. over the churches   D. ad casās
_____5. in the forest   E. in casīs
_____6. near the villa   F. prope insulam
_____7. on the road   G. ad ecclēsiam
_____8. in the forests   H. super terrās
_____9. to the cottages   I. super silvās
_____10. in the churches   J. prope pæninsulam
_____11. near the island   K. in villīs
_____12. over the lands   L. in silvā
_____13. in the villas   M. super ecclēsiās
_____14. to the islands   N. in ecclēsiīs
_____15. near the peninsula   O. prope villam

✏ **F. SENTENCE ELEMENTS PRACTICE** (Identify the underline word in each sentence as a **subject, being verb, intransitive verb, adjective, predicate adjective, predicate nominative, adverb, conjunction, preposition** or **object of a preposition.** Each term is used once.)

1. Rosæ <u>sunt</u> rubræ.   *being verb*
2. <u>Silva</u> est densa.   _____
3. Prope casam puella <u>saltant</u>.   _____
4. Fēminæ cantant <u>in</u> ecclēsiā.   _____
5. Ītalia est <u>pæninsula</u>.   _____
6. Claudia <u>et</u> Octavia sunt puellæ.   _____
7. In <u>silvā</u> columbæ murmurant.   _____
8. Sicilia <u>nōn</u> est pæninsula.   _____
9. Ecclēsia est <u>nōta</u>.   _____
10. <u>Multæ</u> rosæ sunt prope casam.   _____

✏ **G. SENTENCE TRANSLATION** (Translate each sentence.)

1. Columbæ speciōsæ murmurant.

_____

2. Rosæ sunt rubræ et albæ.

_____

3. Ītalia est terra nōta.

_____

4. Silvæ sunt dēnsæ.

_____

5. Familiæ in casīs habitant.

_____

6. Puella bona in ecclēsiā ōrat.

_____

7. Altæ columnæ stant.

_____

8. Nōn sunt opulēntæ.

_____

LESSON FIFTEEN
FIRST DECLENSION MASCULINE NOUNS
(Read p. 38-39 in the reader.)

• **NOUNS** are words which name persons, places, things and ideas. In Latin, nouns are placed in groups called **declensions**. **First declension nouns** are Latin nouns which end in -a in the nominative singular case.

There are only a few masculine first declension nouns.

There are **feminine** and **masculine** nouns in the first declension. Some first declension masculine nouns are **agrıcola, nauta, ıncola, prophēta, poēta** and **patriarcha.**

• **FIRST DECLENSION MASCULINE NOUNS** in **the nominative case** end in -a in the singular and -æ in the plural, just like first declension feminine nouns.

SINGULAR	PLURAL
agricola (farmer)	**agricolæ** (farmers)
nauta (sailor)	**nautæ** (sailors)
incola (inhabitant)	**incolæ** (inhabitant)
patriarcha (patriarch)	**patriārchæ** (patriarchs)

agricola   **nauta**   **incola**   **patriarcha**

✏ **NEW LATIN NOUNS PRACTICE** (Write each.)

incola, -æ, m. *inhabitant* _____

agricola, -æ, m. *farmer* _____

patriarcha, -æ, m. *bishop* _____

✏ **INTRANSITIVE VERBS PRACTICE** (Write each.)

arat *he, she, it plows* _____

arant *they plow* _____

indāgat *he, she, it hunts* _____

indāgant *they hunt* _____

A. SUBJECT-VERB AGREEMENT (Circle the verb which agrees with the underlined subject in each sentence and write on the line.)

1. In terrā **agricola** _arat_.   (a. arat)   b. arant
2. **Agricolæ** _____.   a. arat   b. arant
3. **Aquilæ** super silvam _____.   a. volat   b. volant
4. **Aquila** _____.   a. volat   b. volant
5. **Columba** _____.   a. murmurat   b. murmurant
6. In silvā **columbæ** _____.   a. murmurat   b. murmurant
7. **Puellæ** in silvā _____.   a. saltat   b. saltant
8. **Puella** _____.   a. saltat   b. saltant
9. **Āra** in ecclēsiā _____.   a. stat   b. stant
10. **Columnæ** _____   a. stat   b. stant
11. **Incolæ** in silvā _____.   a. indāgat   b. indāgant
12. **Incola** _____.   a. indāgat   b. indāgant

B. IDENTIFYING FEMININE AND MASCULINE NOUNS (Give the definition of each and circle the correct gender of these first declension nouns.)

1. statua   _statue_   (feminine)   masculine
2. incola   _____   feminine   masculine
3. ancilla   _____   feminine   masculine
4. aquila   _____   feminine   masculine
5. fenestra   _____   feminine   masculine
6. agricola   _____   feminine   masculine
7. āra   _____   feminine   masculine
8. rosa   _____   feminine   masculine
9. silva   _____   feminine   masculine
10. columba   _____   feminine   masculine
11. columna   _____   feminine   masculine
12. ecclēsia   _____   feminine   masculine
13. patriarcha   _____   feminine   masculine
14. casa   _____   feminine   masculine
15. puella   _____   feminine   masculine
16. insula   _____   feminine   masculine
17. pæninsula   _____   feminine   masculine

✎ C. IDENTIFICATION (Underline the being verbs in these sentences.)
1. Puella <u>est</u> Rōmāna.
2. Fēminæ sunt bonæ.
3. Claudia et Octāvia nōn sunt Christiānæ.
4. Est agricola.
5. Sunt ancillæ.
6. In ecclēsiā est patriarcha.
7. Sunt incolæ.
8. Est rosa rubra.
9. Columna est alta.
10. Ītalia est terra antīqua.

✎ D. IDENTIFICATION (Underline each **verb**. Is it **singular** or **plural**?)
1. Incolæ <u>habitant</u> in insulīs.   singular   plural
2. Super silvam aquila volat.   singular   plural
3. Patriārcha in ecclēsiā ōrat.   singular   plural
4. Agrīcola arat.   singular   plural
5. Incolæ indāgant.   singular   plural
6. Lūcia ōrat.   singular   plural
7. In villīs laborant.   singular   plural
8. Cantat.   singular   plural
9. In villā statua pulchra stat.   singular   plural
10. Columbæ murmurant.   singular   plural

✎ E. IDENTIFICATION (Underline each **adjective phrase** and translate.)
1. <u>Columbæ speciōsæ</u> murmurant. *beautiful doves*
2. Aquila magna volat. _____
3. Fenestræ glōriōsæ sunt. _____
4. Altæ columnæ stant. _____
5. In īnsulā nōn sunt silvæ dēnsæ. _____
6. Prope villam sunt rosæ rubræ. _____
7. In viā fēmina bona ambulat. _____
8. Multæ puellæ cantant. _____

71

✎ **F. MISSING PREPOSITIONAL PHRASES** (Fill in the blank with the correct Latin prepositional phrase from the choices below.)

1. Fēminæ *(to the cottages)* ambulant. _____
2. *(In the villas)* ancillæ laborant. _____
3. *(Over the forests)* aquilæ volant. _____
4. *(Near the villas)* statuæ stant. _____
5. Ītalia est *(near the islands)*. _____
6. *(In cottages)* incolæ habitant. _____
7. *(On the land)* agricola arat. _____
8. *(In the forests)* incolæ indāgant. _____
9. *(In the churches)* patriārchæ ōrant. _____
10. Agrīcola *(on the road)* ambulat. _____
11. *(Near the cottage)* sunt rosæ. _____
12. *(Above the land)* aquila volat. _____

prope īnsulās	in casīs	in ecclēsiīs
ad casās	super terram	in silvīs
in villīs	prope villās	super silvās
prope casam	in viā	in terrā

✎ **G. MISSING MACRONS** (Place the macrons where needed in these adjective phrases and translate each.)

1. ecclesia parva _____
2. multæ feminæ _____
3. villa antiqua _____
4. pæninsula nota _____
5. statua gloriosa _____
6. feminæ Christianæ _____
7. familia Romana _____
8. ara splendida _____
9. fenestra gloriosa _____
10. silvæ antiquæ _____

LESSON SIXTEEN

ADJECTIVE PHRASES

Read p. 40-44 in the reader.)

English adjectives are placed **before** the nouns or pronouns they modify, but in Latin the use of adjectives is governed by different rules.

> Adjectives are words which describe nouns or pronouns.

• **ADJECTIVES OF QUALITY** which answer the question *what kind?* are often placed **after** the nouns they modify.

> **columba <u>speciōsa</u>** (a <u>beautiful</u> dove)
>
> **rosa <u>rubra</u>** (the <u>red</u> rose)
>
> **terræ <u>antīquæ</u>** (<u>ancient</u> lands)

rosa rubra

• **ADJECTIVES OF QUANTITY** which answer the question *how many?* are often **before** the nouns they modify.

> **<u>multī</u> nautæ** (many sailors)
>
> **<u>multæ</u> casæ** (many cottages)
>
> **<u>multī</u> virī** (many men)

multæ fēminæ

✏ NEW VOCABULARY (Write each.)

aqua, -æ. f. *water* _____

nauta, -æ, m. *sailor* _____

nāvicula, -æ, f. *little boat* _____

ōra, -æ, f. *shore, beach* _____

poēta, -æ, m. *poet* _____

vita, -æ, f. *life* _____

cæruleus, -a, -um *deep blue* _____

natat *he, she, swims* _____

natant *they swim* _____

nāvigat *he, she, it sails* _____

navigant *they sail* _____

✎ **A. MATCHING** (Match each phrase with its Latin translation.)

___1. aqua cærulea   A. the good maidservant
___2. vita speciōsa   B. a splendid church
___3. viæ rectæ   C. blue water
___4. rosæ rubræ   D. a large eagle
___5. aquila magna   E. small cottages
___6. fenestra glōriōsa   F. Roman women
___7. columbæ albæ   G. the long shore
___8. casæ parvæ   H. white doves
___9. ancilla bona   I. red roses
___10. fēminæ Rōmānæ   J. a beautiful life
___11. nāviculæ albæ   K. dense forest
___12. ōra longa   L. tall columns
___13. silva densa   M. straight roads
___14. ecclēsia splendida   N. glorious window
___15. altæ columnæ   O. white boats

✎ **B. PREPOSITIONAL PHRASES** (Bracket the prepositional phrases.)

1. Nāviculæ [in aquā cæruleā] sunt.
2. In Ītaliā sunt viæ rectæ.
3. Prope casam rosæ albæ sunt.
4. Super silvās aquilæ volant.
5. In terrā agricolæ arant.
6. Prope Ītaliam insula est.
7. In villīs splendidīs familiæ opulēntæ habitant.
8. Āra splendida stat in ecclēsiā.
9. Nautæ sunt in nāviculīs.
10. Ad ecclēsiam puellæ ambulant.
11. In silvā densā columbæ murmurant.
12. In ōrā longā puella saltat.
13. In casīs nautæ habitant.
14. Super aquam aquila volat.
15. Ad villās ancillæ ambulant.

74

C. Subject/Verb Agreement (Which verb agrees with the subject? Circle the best verb in the parentheses.)

1. Alta columna (stat / stant) in villā.
2. Fenestræ (est / sunt) glōriōsæ.
3. In terrā agricolæ (arat / arant).
4. In sīlvīs aquilæ (volat / volant).
5. Aqua (est / sunt) cærulea.
6. Nautæ in aquā (nāvigat / nāvigant).
7. Nāvicula (est / sunt) alba.
8. Puella in ōrā longā (ambulat / ambulant).
9. Fēminæ (cantat / cantant).
10. Patriārcha (ōrat / ōrant).

D. Missing Predicate Nominatives (Add a first declension feminine noun that agrees with the underlined subject.)

1. **Maria et Lūcia sunt** _____.
2. **Ītalia est** _____.
3. **Claudia est** _____.
4. **Sicilia est** _____.
5. **Portia est** _____.

E. Missing Predicate Adjectives (Add a first declension feminine adjective that agrees with the underlined subject.)

1. **Columbæ sunt** _____.
2. **Terra est** _____.
3. **Nāviculæ sunt** _____.
4. **Rosæ sunt** _____.
5. **Āra est** _____.
6. **Ecclēsia est** _____.
7. **Vita est** _____.
8. **Viæ sunt** _____.
9. **Aquilæ sunt** _____.
10. **Aqua est** _____.

F. INTRANSITIVE VERBS (Underline each verb. Is it singular or plural?)

1. Incolæ in silvā indāgant.   singular   plural
2. Super terram āquīla volat.   singular   plural
3. Patriārchæ in ecclēsiīs cantant.   singular   plural
4. Altæ columnæ stant.   singular   plural
5. Poēta in villā splēndidā cantat.   singular   plural
6. In aquā cæruleanatant.   singular   plural
7. Colūmba murmurat.   singular   plural
8. In aquā, nauta nāvigat.   singular   plural
9. Agricolæ arant.   singular   plural
10. Puella parva saltat.   singular   plural

G. IDENTIFY SENTENCE ELEMENTS (Circle the word which describes how each underlined word is being used in the sentence. Sentence elements are listed below. Each term is used once.)

1. In ecclēsiā patriarcha <u>cantat</u>.   *intransitive verb*
2. Vita in Ītaliā est <u>speciōsa</u>.   _____
3. Viæ <u>nōn</u> sunt rectæ.   _____
4. Aqua <u>est</u> cærulea.   _____
5. <u>Agrīcola</u> arat.   _____
6. Super <u>silvās</u> aquilæ volant.   _____
7. <u>Prope</u> casam sunt rosæ.   _____
8. Octāvia est <u>fēmina</u>.   _____
9. Villa nova est <u>splendida</u>.   _____
10. Maria <u>et</u> Lūcia sunt ancillæ.   _____

| preposition | being verb | adverb |
| object of a preposition | ~~intransitive verb~~ | conjunction |

| predicate nominative | subject |
| predicate adjective | adjective |

LESSONS 13-16 REVIEW

PART I. CONCEPT AND VOCABULARY REVIEW

A. GRAMMAR REVIEW (Circle the correct word in the parentheses.)

1. (Singular / Plural) nouns refer to more than one person, place or thing.

2. (Singular / Plural) nouns refer to one person, place or thing

3. An (adjective / adverb) is a word which describes a noun or pronoun.

4. Est is a (singular / plural) being verb.

5. Sunt is a (singular / plural) being verb.

6. (Nouns / Prepositions) are words that name persons, places or things.

7. The first declension nominative singular ending is (-a / -æ).

8. The first declension nominative plural ending is (-a / -æ).

9. Latin nouns are placed in groups called (declensions / conjugations).

10. Most first declension nouns are (feminine / masculine.)

11. The (subject / preposition) is the person, place or thing the sentence is about.

12. (In / Ad) may be translated as *in, on* or *upon*.

13. Nōn is an (adverb / adjective).

14. Et is a (conjunction / preposition) which joins words together.

15. In is a (conjunction / preposition) showing a relationship between words.

16. First declension masculine nouns in the nominative case (do / do not end) in -a in the singular and -æ in the plural, just like first declension feminine nouns.

17. Adjectives of quality are usually placed (before / after) nouns they modify.

18. Latin adjectives (must / must not) agree with the nouns they modify in case, number and gender.

19. Intransitive verbs (do / do not) require an object to complete their meaning.

20. Ōrat, cantat and ambulat are (intransitive / being) verbs.

21. Third person (singular / plural) verbs end in -nt.

22. Present tense means the action is happening (now / in the future.)

23. Predicate (nominatives / adjectives) are nouns or pronouns which follow a being verb and rename or describe the subject.

24. Predicate (nominatives /adjectives) are adjectives which follow a being verb and rename or describe the subject.

25. "Third person" means the (subject / verb) is being spoken about.

B. FIRST DECLENSION NOUNS (Define and circle correct gender.)

1. **aqua** _____ feminine masculine
2. **aquila** _____ feminine masculine
3. **āra** _____ feminine masculine
4. **terra** _____ feminine masculine
5. **columba** _____ feminine masculine
6. **fenestra** _____ feminine masculine
7. **ōra** _____ feminine masculine
8. **nāvicula** _____ feminine masculine
9. **rosa** _____ feminine masculine
10. **vita** _____ feminine masculine
11. **agricola** _____ feminine masculine
12. **nauta** _____ feminine masculine
13. **incola** _____ feminine masculine
14. **patriarcha** _____ feminine masculine
15. **poēta** _____ feminine masculine

C. ADJECTIVES (Define.)

1. **albus, -a, -um** _____
2. **altus, -a, -um** _____
3. **antīquus, -a, -um** _____
4. **cæruleus, -a, -um** _____
5. **densus, -a, -um** _____
6. **magnus, -a, -um** _____
7. **multus, -a, -um** _____
8. **novus, -a. -um** _____
9. **opulentus, -a, -um** _____
10. **rectus, -a, -um** _____
11. **rubrus, -a, -um** _____
12. **speciōsus, -a, -um** _____

D. BEING VERBS REVIEW (Translate each.)
1. est   _____
2. sunt   _____

E. PREPOSITIONS REVIEW (Translate each.)
1. in   _____
2. ad   _____
3. prope   _____
4. super   _____

F. CONJUNCTION REVIEW (Translate each.)
1. et   _____

G. ADVERB REVIEW (Translate each.)
1. nōn   _____

H. PREPOSITIONAL PHRASES REVIEW (Translate each.)
1. in villā   _____
2. in casā   _____
3. ad ecclēsiam   _____
4. prope insulam   _____
5. prope Ītaliam   _____
6. prope casam   _____
7. in terrā   _____
8. in ōrā   _____
9. in aquā   _____
10. in villā splēndidā   _____
11. in casā parvā   _____
12. in silvā densā   _____
13. super silvās   _____
14. in casīs   _____
15. in nāviculīs   _____
16. in aquā cærulea   _____

I. INTRANSITVE VERBS (Give a definition for each verb.)

1. **arat** _____
2. **arant** _____
3. **cantat** _____
4. **cantant** _____
5. **habitat** _____
6. **habitant** _____
7. **indāgat** _____
8. **indāgant** _____
9. **murmurat** _____
10. **murmurant** _____
11. **natat** _____
12. **natant** _____
13. **nāvigat** _____
14. **nāvigant** _____
15. **saltat** _____
16. **saltant** _____
17. **stāt** _____
18. **stant** _____
19. **volat** _____
20. **volant** _____

PART II. PRACTICAL APPLICATION

J. FORMING NOMINATIVE PLURALS (Make these nouns plural.)
1. fenestra   _____
2. columba   _____
3. nauta   _____
4. insula   _____

K. SUBJECTS AND VERBS (Do the subject and verb agree?)
1. <u>Colūmbæ</u> murmurant in silvīs.   Yes ____ No ____
2. In terrā <u>agricolæ</u> lāborat.   Yes ____ No ____
3. <u>Nautæ</u> est in nāviculīs.   Yes ____ No ____
4. <u>Vita</u> est speciōsa in Ītaliā antīquā.   Yes ____ No ____
5. <u>Puellæ</u> in aquā natant.   Yes ____ No ____

L. SUBJECT/VERB AGREEMENT (Circle the correct verb.)
1. Nautæ (nāvigat / nāvigant).
2. Fenestra (est / sunt) glōriōsa.
3. In ōrā puellæ (saltat / saltant).
4. Super silvās aquila (volat / volant).
5. Columnæ (est / sunt) altæ.

M. PREDICATE NOMINATIVE/ADJECTIVE IDENTIFICATION (Is the underlined word a predicate nominative or a predicate adjective?)
1. Aqua est <u>cærulea</u>. _____
2. Rōsa est <u>alba</u>. _____
3. Fēminæ sunt <u>opulēntæ</u>. _____
4. Portia est <u>ancilla</u>. _____
5. Nauta est <u>incola</u>. _____
6. Columnæ sunt <u>altæ</u>. _____
7. Sicilia est <u>insula</u>. _____
8. Ītalia est <u>pæninsula</u>. _____
9. Familia est <u>Rōmāna</u>. _____
10. Terræ sunt <u>antīquæ</u>. _____

N. PREPOSITIONAL PHRASE IDENTIFICATION (Place brackets around each prepositional phrase and write on line.)

1. [In casā parvā] puella habitat. _in the small cottage_

2. In ecclēsiā altæ columnæ stant. _____

3. Aquila volat super silvās. _____

4. In silvā densā columba murmurat. _____

5. In viā longā ancillæ ambulant. _____

O. MATCHING (Match the adjective phrases with correct English translations.)

____1. rosa rubra   A. the blue water
____2. fenestræ glōriōsæ   B. white boats
____3. āra splendida   C. a dense forest
____4. puellæ Rōmānæ   D. the famous peninsula
____5. silva densa   E. a large eagle
____6. aqua cærulea   F. beautiful doves
____7. viæ rectæ   G. many sailors
____8. villæ novæ   H. a splendid altar
____9. columbæ speciōsæ   I. straight roads
____10. aquila magna   J. beautiful statue
____11. nāviculæ albæ   K. Roman girls
____12. multæ nautæ   L. ancient land
____13. statua pulchra   M. red rose
____14. pæninsula nōta   N. new villas
____15. terra antīqua   O. glorious windows

P. SENTENCE TRANSLATION (Translate each sentence.)

1. In ecclēsiā cantant et ōrant.

_____

2. Viæ in Siciliā nōn sunt longæ.

_____

3. Ītalia est terra Christiāna.

_____

4. Rosæ sunt albæ et rubræ.

_____

5. Incolæ in pæninsulā habitant.

_____

Q. PREPOSITIONAL PHRASES (Place brackets around <u>prepositional phrases</u>.)
1. Nāviculæ [in aquā cæruleā] sunt.
2. In Siciliā nōn sunt viæ rectæ.
3. Prope casam rosæ rubræ sunt.
4. Super silvam aquilæ volant.
5. In terrā agricola arat.
6. Prope Italīam insula est.
7. In villā splēndidā familia opulenta habitat.
8. Altæ columnæ stant in ecclēsiā.
9. Nauta est in navīculā.
10. Ad ecclēsiam puellæ ambulant.

R. INTRANSITIVE VERBS (Underline the **verb**. Is it **singular** or **plural**?)
1. Īncola in silvā indāgat.   singular   plural
2. Super silvās aquilæ volant.   singular   plural
3. Patriārcha in ecclēsiā cantat.   singular   plural
4. Altæ columnæ stant.   singular   plural
5. Poēta in villā splēndidā cantat. singular   plural

S. PROOFREADING (Draw a line each spelling mistakes and write corrected word.)
1. Agrecola arat.   _____
2. Prope casam colmbae murmurant.   _____
3. In Siciliā oest Mons Ætna.   _____
4. Fēminæ bonæ āmbulornt.   _____
5. Sunt Multæ ecclisiæ in Ītaliā.   _____
6. Rosæ sunt albæ et rubraie.   _____

ANSWER KEY

Lesson One
A. Grammar Questions, p. 2
1. Nouns
2. declensions
3. First

B. Identification, p. 2
1. fēmina
2. puella

C. Matching, p. 2
1. puella (girl)
2. fēmina (woman)

D. English-to-Latin, p. 2
1. girl (puella)
2. woman (fēmina)

F. Latin Vowels Practice, p. 3
1. "oh"
2. "ee"
3. "ah"
4. "eh"
5. "oo"
6. in between "eh" and "ay"
7. "ay"

H. Latin Consonants Practice, p. 4
1. "ny
2. "ch"
1. "z"
4. "tsee"
5. "k"
6. "g" as in "generation"

Lesson Two
A. English Practice, p. 5
1. boy, singular
2. Rome, singular
3. geese, plural
4. lake, singular
5. boys, plural
6. Roses, plural
7. Ann, singular
8. Stars, plural

B. Grammar Questions, p. 6
1. subject
2. singular
3. plural
4. being
5. singular
6. Nouns
7. declensions
8. First
9. common
10. proper

C. Latin Practice, p. 6
1. a. She is not a woman.
2. b. She is a maidservant.
3. b. Lucy is a girl.
4. a. Maria is a woman.

D. English-to-Latin, p. 6
1. girl (puella)
2. woman (fēmina)
3. maidservant (ancilla)

E. Subject-Verb Agreement, p. 7
1. is (singular)
2. are (plural)
3. is (singular)
4. are (plural)
5. is (singular)
6. is (singular)
7. is (singular)
8. is (singular)

F. Proper and Common Nouns, p. 7
1. Lūcia (proper)
2. ancilla (common)
3. Maria (proper)
4. fēmina (common)
5. puella (common)

G. Missing Macrons, p. 7
1. puella
2. fēmina
3. ancilla
4. Maria
5. Lūcia
6. nōn

H. Proofreading, p. 7
1. ~~ancīla~~   ancilla
2. ~~Eit~~   Est
3. ~~fæmina~~   fēmina
4. pueela   puella
4. ~~nūon~~   nōn
5. ~~Lūcie~~   Lūcia

I. Name the Picture, p. 8
1. fēmina
2. puella
3. ancilla

J. English-To-Latin, p. 8
1. Est fēmina.
2. Est ancilla.
3. Est puella.
4. Nōn est ancilla.
5. Nōn est puella.
6. Nōn est fēmina.
7. Lūcia est puella.
8. Maria est fēmina.
9. Lūcia nōn est ancilla.
10. Maria nōn est puella.

Lesson Three
A. Subject/Adjective Identification, p. 10
1. Fēmina est pulchra. (The woman is beautiful.)
2. Lūcia est Rōmāna. (Lucia is Roman.)
3. Puella nōn est opulenta. (The girl is not wealthy.)
4. Octāvia est Christiāna. (Octavia is Christian.)
5. Ancilla est bona. (The maidservant is good.)

B. Grammar Questions, p. 10
1. adjective
2. subject
3. singular
4. plural
5. singular
6. Nouns
7. declensions
8. First
9. common
10. proper

C. Matching Sentences, p. 10
1. Fēmina est bona.
2. Puella nōn est pulchra.
3. Est Rōmāna.
4. Fēmina est pulchra.
5. Puella est Rōmāna.
6. Est opulenta.
7. Fēmina nōn est Christiāna.
8. Est parva.
9. Ancilla est bona.

B. The woman is good.
I. The girl is not pretty.
A. She is Roman.
C. The woman is pretty.
E. The girl is Roman.
D. She is wealthy.
G. The woman is not Christian.
F. She is small.
H. The maidservant is good.

D. Adjectives Practice, p. 11
1. Octāvia est (opulenta, bona, Rōmāna, Christiāna, pulchra, parva).
2. Puella est (opulenta, bona, Rōmāna, Christiāna, pulchra, parva)
3. Claudia est (opulenta, bona, Rōmāna, Christiāna, pulchra, parva)
4. Ancilla nōn est (opulenta, bona, Rōmāna, Christiāna, pulchra, parva)
5. Lūcia est (opulenta, bona, Rōmāna, Christiāna, pulchra, parva).
6. Fēmina nōn est (opulenta, bona, Rōmāna, Christiāna, pulchra, parva).
7. Maria est (opulenta, bona, Rōmāna, Christiāna, pulchra, parva).
8. Puella nōn est (opulenta, bona, Rōmāna, Christiāna, pulchra, parva).

E. Subjects Practice, p. 11
1. (Fēmina, Puella, Ancilla, Claudia, Lūcia, Portia, Octāvia, Maria) est pulchra.
2. (Fēmina, Puella, Ancilla, Claudia, Lūcia, Portia, Octāvia, Maria) nōn est opulenta.
3. (Fēmina, Puella, Ancilla, Claudia, Lūcia, Portia, Octāvia, Maria) est Christiāna.
4. (Fēmina, Puella, Ancilla, Claudia, Lūcia, Portia, Octāvia, Maria) est bona.
5. (Fēmina, Puella, Ancilla, Claudia, Lūcia, Portia, Octāvia, Maria) nōn est Rōmāna.
6. (Fēmina, Puella, Ancilla, Claudia, Lūcia, Portia, Octāvia, Maria) nōn est parva.
7. (Fēmina, Puella, Ancilla, Claudia, Lūcia, Portia, Octāvia, Maria) est opulenta.

F. Subject/Adjective Practice, p. 12
1. Fēmina is the subject. (The woman is wealthy.)
2. Lūcia is the subject. (Lucia is pretty.)
3. Christiāna is an adjective. (The girl is Christian.)
4. Octāvia is the subject. (Octavia is not Roman.)
5. Ancilla is the subject. (The maidservant is good.)
6. Puella is the subject. (The girl is pretty.)
7. Rōmāna is an adjective. (Lūcia is Roman.)
8. Ancilla is the subject. (The maidservant is Christian.)

G. True or False, p. 12
1. True.
2. False. A noun names a person, place, thing, or idea.
3. True.
4. True.
5. False. First declension nouns end in -a in the nominative singular.
6. True.
7. False. A subject is singular if it is one person, place or thing.
8. True.

H. Missing Macrons, p. 12
1. bona (good)
2. pulchra (pretty, beautiful)
3. Christiāna (Christian)
4. Rōmāna (Roman)
5. Lūcia (Lucia)
6. opulenta (wealthy)
7. nōn (not)

I. Proper and Common Nouns, p. 12

1. Claudia (proper)
2. puella (common)
3. fēmina (common)
4. Lūcia (proper)
5. Maria (proper)
6. ancilla (common)
7. Octāvia (proper)
8. Portia (proper)

Lesson Four
A. Plural Practice, p. 14

1. fēmina, fēminæ (woman, women)
2. puella, puellæ (girl, girls)
3. villa, villæ (manor, manors)
4. ecclēsia, ecclēsiæ (church, churches)
5. vīa, viæ (road, roads)

6. ancilla, ancillæ (maid, maids)
7. silva, silvæ (forest, forests)
8. casa, casæ (cottage, cottages)
9. familia, famīliæ (family, families)

B. Subject/Adjective Identification, p. 14

1. Puella est pulchra. (The girl is pretty.)
2. Casa est parva. (The cottage is small.)
3. Claudia est opulenta. (Claudia is wealthy.)
4. Lūcia est Christiāna. (Lucia is Christian.)

D. Matching, p. 15

1. D. the pretty girls
2. A. the small cottage
3. G. the opulent villa
4. H. Christian women
5. B. a good maidservant
6. C. Roman roads
7. E. the Christian church
8. F. a Roman girl

E. Adjective Practice, p. 15

1. Fēmina est (opulenta, bona, Rōmāna, Christiāna, pulchra, parva).
2. Casa est parva.
3. Portia est (opulenta, bona, Rōmāna, Christiāna, pulchra, parva).
4. Villa nōn est (opulenta, pulchra, parva).
5. Lūcia nōn est (opulenta, bona, Rōmāna, Christiāna, pulchra, parva).
6. Puella est (opulenta, bona, Rōmāna, Christiāna, pulchra, parva)
7. Vīa est (Romana, longa).
8. Silva est (parva, pulchra).
9. Ecclēsia est (opulenta, Rōmāna, Christiāna, pulchra, parva).
10. Ancilla nōn est (opulenta, bona, Rōmāna, Christiāna, parva).

F. Missing Macrons, p. 15
1. fēmina (woman)
2. ecclēsia (church)
3. Christiāna (Christian)
4. Lūcia (Lucia)
5. Rōmāna (Roman)
6. Octāvia (Octavia)

G. Subject-Adjective Identification, p. 16
1. Vīa is the subject. (The road is long.)
2. Portia is the subject. (Portia is pretty.)
3. Rōmāna is the predicate adjective. (The woman is Roman.)
4. Villa is the subject. (The villa is opulent.)
5. Bona is the predicate adjective. (The maidservant is good.)
6. Christiāna is the predicate adjective. (The girl is Christian.)
7. Rōmāna is the predicate adjective. (Maria is not Roman.)
8. Silva is the subject. (The forest is small.)
9. Ecclēsia is the subject. (The church is Christian.)
10. Fēmina is the subject. (The woman is good.)

H. Proofreading, p. 16
1. ~~longe~~   longa   (The road is long.)
2. ~~Famīllia~~   Familia   (The family is Christian.)
3. ~~Ecclisia~~   Ecclēsia   (The church is not small.)
4. ~~eest~~   est   (She is not Octavia.)
5. ~~Silvo~~   Silva   (The forest is small.)
6. ~~opullenta~~   opulenta   (The villa is opulent.)

I. Name the Picture, p. 16
1. ecclēsia (church)
2. familia (family)
3. puella (girl)
4. ancilla (maidservant)

Lesson 1-4 Review, p. 17
A. Grammar Review
1. Plural
2. Singular
3. adjective
4. singular
5. Nouns
6. -ā
7. -æ
8. declensions
9. feminine
10. subject
11. adverb

B. First Declension Noun Review, p. 17
1. maidservant
2. cottage
3. church
4. woman
5. girl
6. forest
7. road
8. manor
9. family

C. Adjective Review, p. 17
1. good
2. Christian
3. long
4. wealthy, opulent
5. pretty, beautiful
6. Roman

D. Being Verbs Review, p. 17
1. (he, she, it) is
2. (they) are

Part II. Practical Application, p. 18
E. Forming Plurals
1. fēminæ (women)
2. puellæ (girls)
3. villæ (manors)
4. ecclēsiæ (churches)
5. viæ (roads)
6. ancillæ (maidservants)
7. silvæ (forests)
8. casæ (cottages)
9. famīliæ (families)

F. Subject/Predicate Adjective Identification, p. 18

1. <u>Fēmina</u> est Christiāna. (The woman is Christian.)

2. <u>Casa</u> nōn est opulenta. (The cottage is not opulent.)

3. <u>Octāvia</u> est Rōmāna. (Octavia is Roman.)

4. <u>Vīa</u> est longa. (The road is long.)

5. <u>Claudia</u> est pulchra. (Claudia is pretty.)

G. Adjective Review, p. 18
1. She is good.
2. The family is wealthy.
3. Portia is a girl.
4. The maidservant is Christian.
5. The church is not small.

Lesson Five
A. Latin Practice, p. 20
1. Maria <u>est</u> puella. (Mary is a girl.)
2. Claudia <u>est</u> fēmina. (Claudia is a woman.)
3. Ancilla <u>est</u> bona. (The maidservant is good.)
4. Lucīa et Octāvia <u>sunt</u> Rōmānæ. (Lucy and Octavia are Roman.)
5. Puellæ <u>sunt</u> Christiānæ. (The girls are Christian.)

B. Name the Picture, p. 20
1. b. fēmina
2. a. fēminæ
3. a. Lūcia et Maria
4. a. puella et fēmina
5. a. puella
6. b. puellæ

C. Plural Subjects, p. 21
1. Fēminæ sunt opulēntæ. (The women are wealthy.)
2. Claudia et Octāvia sunt Rōmānæ. (Claudia and Octavia are Roman.)
3. Ancillæ sunt bonæ. (The maidservants are good.)
4. Lūcia et Maria sunt puellæ. (Lucia and Maria are girls.)
5. Fēminæ sunt Chritiānæ. (The women are Christian.)
6. Viæ sunt longæ. (The roads are long.)
7. Silvæ nōn sunt parvæ. (The forests are not small.)
8. Puellæ sunt pūlchræ. (The girls are beautiful.)

D. Matching, p. 21
1. I. small cottages
2. C. opulent villas
3. H. a good family
4. F. Roman roads
5. J. the good maidservant
6. A. small forest
7. E. the Christian churches
8. G. the Roman girls
9. B. a long road
10. D. a pretty woman

E. Subject/Predicate Adjective Identification, p. 21

1. Silva is the subject. (The forest is small.)
2. Lūcia is the subject. (Lucia is good.)
3. Christiāna is the predicate adjective. (The girl is Christian.)
4. Claudia is the subject. (Claudia is wealthy.)
5. Rōmāna is the predicate adjective. (The family is not Roman.)

F. Parts of Speech, p. 22

1. (cottage) noun
2. (not) adverb
3. (wealthy) adjective
4. (and) conjunction
5. (they are) being verb
6. (small) adjective
7. (forest) noun
8. (he, she, it is) being verb
9. (church) noun
10. (long) adjective

G. English-to-Latin, p. 22

1. Portia est Rōmāna.
2. Familia est Christiāna.
3. Maria et Lūcia sunt puellæ.
4. Fēmina est bona.
5. Viæ sunt longæ.
6. Octāvia et Claudia sunt fēminæ.
7. Ancilla est bona.
8. Ecclēsia nōn est parva.

Lesson Six
A. Adjective Practice, p. 23

1. the small town
2. a good boy
3. the enormous ship
4. the magnificent cathedral
5. the yellow sun
6. a steep hill
7. the busy town
8. an ancient wall

B. Latin Practice, p. 24

1. a. Fēmina est bona.
2. a. Puella est pulchra.
3. b. Fēminæ sunt Rōmānæ
4. a. Lūcia est Rōmāna.

93

C. Verb Practice, p. 24

No. 1. <u>Puellae</u> **sunt** bonæ. (The girls are good.)
Yes. 2. (The woman is wealthy.)
No. 3. Lucia **est** Rōmāna. (Lucia is Roman.)
Yes. 4. (Lucīa and Octāvia are Roman.)
No. 5. Puella et fēmina **sunt** bonæ. (The woman and girl are good.)
No. 6. Lucīa et Portia **sunt** bonæ. (Lucia and Portia are good.)
No. 7. Fēminæ **sunt** Christiānæ. (The women are Christian.)
Yes. 8. (The girl is good.)

D. Noun /Adjective Identification, p. 25

1. noun (It is a Christian church.)
2. adjective (Antonia is a good woman.)
3. noun (They are opulent villas.)
4. noun (The Roman girl is Claudia.)
5. adjective (Maria is a good maidservant.)
6. adjective (Octavia is a wealthy woman.)
7. adjective (The pretty girl is Lucia.)
8. noun (It is a small cottage.)

E. Missing Adjectives, p. 25

1. pulchra (The pretty girl is Maria.)
2. Rōmānæ (Claudia and Octavia are Roman girls.)
3. Christiānæ (They are Christian women.)
4. bona (Antonia is a good woman.)
5. Rōmāna (Maria is not Roman woman.)
6. longæ (There are long roads.)
7. Christiānæ (They are Christian churches.)
8. parva (It is a small forest.)

F. Missing Being Verbs, p. 25

1. sunt (Portia and Lucia are Roman girls.)
2. sunt (Claudia and Octavia are wealthy.)
3. est (The girl is good.)
4. sunt (The roads are long.)
5. est (Maria is a Christian woman.)
6. sunt (The churches are not small.)
7. est (The villa is opulent.)

G. Proper and Common Nouns, p. 26

1. common
2. proper
3. common
4. proper
5. common
6. common
7. common
8. proper
9. proper
10. common

94

H. Proofreading, p. 26

1. ~~pellae~~	puellae	(Octavia and Claudia are Roman girls.)
2. ~~femna~~	fēmina	(Antonia is a Christian woman.)
3. ~~long~~	longa	(The road is long.)
4. ~~Cassa~~	casa	(The cottage is small.)
5. ~~Eclesiæ~~	Ecclēsiæ	(The churches are Christian.)
6. ~~opulentar~~	opulenta	(The villa is opulent.)
7. ~~Ancila~~	Ancilla	(The maidservant is good.)
8. ~~pulcra~~	pulchra	(Octavia is pretty.)

I. Adjective Phrases, p. 26

1. fēmina bona
2. fēminæ bonæ
3. ecclēsia Christiāna
4. ecclēsiæ Christiānæ
5. casa parva
6. casæ parvæ

Lesson Seven
A. Grammar Questions, p. 27

1. In may be translated as in, on or upon.
2. Sunt is a plural being verb.
3. Est is a singular being verb.
4. The first declension ending æ is plural.
5. The first declension ending ā is singular.
6. Nōn is an adverb.
7. Et is a conjunction which joins words together.
8. In is a preposition showing relationship between words.
9. *In silvā* is a prepositional phrase.
10. Adjectives of quality are usually placed after the nouns they modify.
11. A common noun denotes a class of objects.
12. A proper noun names a specific person, place, thing or idea, spelled with a beginning capital letter.

B. English Practice, p. 28

1. b. Fēminæ sunt in villā.
2. b. Sunt Christiānæ.
3. b. Puellæ nōn sunt Rōmānæ.

C. Matching, p. 28

1. D. a good girl
2. F. the beautiful church
3. B. the pretty girl
4. H. a Roman girl
5. A. the Roman woman
6. G. the Christian girl
7. C. a wealthy woman
8. E. a small cottage

D. Name the Picture, p. 28 (Some possibilities.)
1. Fēminæ sunt Rōmānæ.
2. Puellæ sunt bonæ.

E. Subject/Verb Agreeement, p. 29
1. Sunt (The girls are on the road.)
2. Sunt (There are women in the villa.)
3. Est (The maidservant is in the cottage.)
4. est (The woman is in the church.)
5. sunt (The girls are in the forest.)

F. Parts of Speech, p. 29
1. silva (forest)	noun
2. in (in, on, upon)	preposition
3. pulchra (pretty)	adjective
4. est (is)	being verb
5. et (and)	conjunction
6. opulenta (wealthy)	adjective
7. nōn (not)	adverb
8. sunt (are)	being verb
9. fēmina (woman)	noun
10. bona (good)	adjective
11. longa (long)	adjective
12. puella (girl)	noun
13. parva (small)	adjective
14. Portia	noun
15. Rōmāna (Roman)	adjective

G. Missing Macrons, p. 29
1. in viā (on the road)
2. in casā (in the cottage)
3. in silvā (in the forest)
4. in ecclēsiā (in the church)
5. in villā (in the villa)

H. Nominative Endings, p. 30
1. silvæ
2. ecclēsia
3. vīā
4. puellæ
5. villæ
6. fēmina
7. ancillæ
8. casæ
9. familia

D. Missing Adjectives, p. 30

1. Portia est (pulchra, Rōmāna, bona, opulenta, Christiāna, parva).
2. Claudia et Octāvia sunt (pūlchræ, Rōmānæ, bonæ, opulēntæ, Christiānæ, parvæ).
3. Antōnia est (pulchra, Rōmāna, bona, opulenta, Christiāna, parva).
4. Lūcia et Antōnia sunt (pūlchræ, Rōmānæ, bonæ, opulēntæ, Christiānæ, parvæ).
5. Maria est (pulchra, Rōmāna, bona, opulenta, Christiāna, parva).
6. Maria et Portia sunt (pūlchræ, Rōmānæ, bonæ, opulēntæ, Christiānæ, parvæ).
7. Ecclēsia est (pulchra, Rōmāna, bona, opulenta, Christiāna, parva).
8. Ecclēsiæ sunt (pūlchræ, Rōmānæ, bonæ, opulēntæ, Christiānæ, parvæ).
9. Vīa est (Rōmāna, longa).
10. Viæ sunt (Rōmānæ, longæ).
11. Casa est parva.
12. Casæ sunt parvæ.

Lesson Eight
A. Intransitive Verb Practice, p. 32
1. F. She walks.
2. C. She prays.
3. A. The girl walks on the road.
4. D. The woman sings.
5. B. The girl walks in the forest.
6. E. The girl walks to the church.

B. Being Verb Practice, p. 32
1. Ecclēsia est splendida. (The church is splendid.)
2. Fēmina et puella sunt bonæ. (The woman and girl are good.)
3. Octāvia et Claudia sunt opulēntæ. (Octavia and Claudia are wealthy.)

C. Adjective Phrase Practice, p. 32
1. A. vīa antīqua (the ancient road)
2. B. ecclēsia antīqua (an ancient church)
3. B. fēmina Rōmāna (a Roman woman)

D. Missing Adjectives, p. 33
1. antīqua (The church is ancient.)
2. longæ (The roads are long.)
3. magna (The forest is large.)
4. splendidæ (The villas are splendid.)
5. bonæ (The women are good.)
6. parva (The cottage is small.)
7. Rōmāna (The girl is Roman.)
8. Rōmānæ (The maidservants are not Roman.)
9. Christiānæ (The families are Christian.)
10. opulenta (Octavia is wealthy.)

E. Missing Intransitive Verbs, p. 33

1. cantat, ōrat (In the church Lucia sings or prays.)
2. ambulat (The maid walks to the villa.)
3. ambulat (A woman walks on the road.)
4. cantat (In the villa Claudia sings.)
5. ambulat (The girl walks to the church.)
6. ōrat, cantat (The family prays or sings in the church.)
7. ambulat (The girl walks to the cottage.)
8. ambulat (Antonia walks on the road.)

F. Subject/Verb Agreement, p. 33

1. No. Antōnia et Maria cantant. (Antonia and Mary sing.)
2. Yes. (The woman walks.)
3. Yes. (The villas are splendid.)
4. Yes. (The church is ancient.)
5. No. Silvæ sunt magnæ. (The forests are large.)
6. Yes. (Lucia prays.)
7. No. Fēmina et puella ambulant. (A woman and girl walk.)
8. Yes. (Portia sings)
9. No. Casa nōn est magna. (The cottage is not large.)
10. Yes. (Claudia is pretty.)

G. Matching, p. 34

1. H. puellæ bonæ
2. E. ecclēsia antīqua
3. C. viæ longæ
4. K. puellæ Rōmānæ
5. B. villa magna
6. I. fāmilia opulenta
7. G. vīa antīqua
8. J. casæ parvæ
9. F. ecclēsiæ splendidæ
10. L. ancilla bona
11. D. famīliæ Christīanæ
12. A. fēminæ Rōmānæ

H. Parts of Speech, p. 34

1. ad (toward)	preposition
2. fēmina (woman)	noun
3. ōrat (he, she, it prays)	intransitive verb
4. est (he, she, it is)	being verb
5. magna (large)	adjective
6. opulenta (opulent, wealthy)	adjective
7. nōn (not)	adverb
8. ambulat (he, she, it walks)	intransitive verb
9. in (in, on, upon)	preposition
10. sunt (they are)	being verb

H. Parts of Speech, p. 34 (continued)

11. Lūcia   noun
12. puella (girl)   noun
13. antīqua (ancient, old)   adjective
14. silva (forest)   noun
15. Rōmāna (Roman)   adjective

Lessons 1-8 Review, p. 35
A. Grammar Questions, p. 35

1. Plural
2. Singular
3. adjective
4. singular
5. plural
6. Nouns
7. -a
8. -æ
9. declensions
10. feminine
11. subect
12. In
13. adverb
14. conjunction
15. preposition
16. prepositional phrase
17. after
18. must
19. do not
20. intransitive

B. First Declension Noun Review, p. 35

1. maidservant
2. cottage
3. church
4. woman
5. girl
6. forest
7. road
8. villa, manor

C. Adjective Review, p. 36

1. ancient, old
2. good
3. Christian
4. long
5. large
6. opulent, wealthy
7. beautiful, pretty
8. splendid

D. Being Verb Review, p. 36

1. he, she it is
2. they are

E. Intransitive Verb Review, p. 36

1. he, she, it walks
2. he, she, it sings
3. he, she, it prays

F. Prepositional Review, p. 36

1. in, on, upon (with ablative)
2. to, toward (with accusative)

G. Conjunction Review, p. 36

1. and

99

I. Prepositional Phrases Review, p. 36
1. in villā (in the villa)
2. in casā (in the cottage)
2. ad ecclēsiam (to the church)

Part II. Practical Application
J. Forming Plurals, p. 37
1. fēmina, fēminæ
2. puella, puellæ
3. villa, villæ
4. ecclēsia, ecclēsiæ

5. vīa, viæ
6. ancilla, ancillæ
7. silva, silvæ
8. casa, casæ

K. Subject/Verb Agreement, p. 37
1. Ancilla est bona. (The maidservant is good.)
2. Claudia et Octāvia sunt Rōmānæ. (Claudia and Octavia are Roman.)
3. Puella est pulchra. (The girl is pretty.)
4. Lucīa est Christiāna. (Lucia is Christian.)
5. Fēminæ nōn sunt opulēntæ. (The women are not wealthy.)
6. Villa est splendida. (The villa is splendid.)
7. Portia et Antōnia sunt Christiānæ. (Portia and Antonia are Christian.)
8. Vīa antīqua est longa. (The ancient road is long.)

L. Verb Practice, p. 37
1. Yes. The girl is good.
2. No. Ancillæ is plural and est is singular. (Should be: Ancilla nōn est Romana.)
3. No. Portia is singular; sunt is plural. (Should be: Portia est Romana.)
4. Yes. Lucīa and Octāvia are pretty.
5. Yes. Puella is plural and ambulat is singular.
6. Yes. Lucia prays.
7. Yes. The women are Christian.
8. Yes. The maidservant is good.
9. No. Silva is singular and sunt is plural. (Should be: Silva est magna.)

M. Subject/Adjective, p. 38
1. Fēmina est Christiāna. (The woman is Christian.)
2. Casæ non sunt splendidæ. (The cottages are not splendid.)
3. Octāvia est opulenta. (Octavia is wealthy.)
4. Viæ sunt longæ. (The roads are long.)
5. Claudia est pulchra. (Claudia is beautiful.)

N. Prepositional Phrases, p. 38
1. In vīā (The women and girls walk on the road.)
2. in villā (The maidservant works in the villa.)
3. ad ecclēsiam (Lucia walks to the church.)
4. in casā (The girls in the cottage sing.)
5. In ecclēsiā (In the church the good woman prays.)

O. Matching, p. 38
1. D. a good maidservant (ancilla bona)
2. I. splendid churches (ecclēsiæ splendidae)
3. B. the pretty girl (puella pulchra)
4. A. the Roman women (fēminae Rōmānae)
5. H. a large forest (silva magna)
6. E. small cottages (casae parvae)
7. C. a wealthy woman (fēmina opulenta)
8. J. long roads (vīae longae)
9. G. the opulent villas (villae opulentae)
10. F. an ancient church (ecclēsia antīqua)

P. Sentence Practice, p. 38
1. They (feminine) are good.
2. The ancient road is long.
3. Antonia prays in the church.
4. The girls are in the cottage.
5. The church is splendid.

Lesson Nine
A. Subject-Verb Agreement, p. 40
1. a. Fēmina ōrat. (The woman prays.)
2. b. Familia ambulat. (The family walks.)
3. b. Puella cantat. (The girl sings.)
4. a. Aquila magna volat. (The eagle flies.)
5. b. Puella saltat. (The girl dances.)

B. Latin Practice, p. 40
1. The family is Christian.
2. The Roman girl walks.
3. She prays.
4. A woman sings in the cottage.
5. Octavia walks to the country manor.
6. The church is Christian.
7. Lucia and Maria are good.
8. The girl dances.
9. The great eagle flies.
10. The roads are ancient.

C. Practice with Plurals, p. 40
1. puellæ bonæ (the good girls)
2. famīliæ Christiānæ (Christian families)
3. ecclēsiæ novæ (the new churches)
4. viæ longæ (the long roads)
5. viæ rectæ (straight roads)
6. aquilæ magnæ (large eagles)
7. villæ splendidæ (splendid villas)
8. casæ parvæ (small cottages)

D. English-to-Latin, p. 41
1. Portia cantat.
2. Ōrat.
3. Octāvia saltat.
4. Fēmina ambulat.
5. Puella cantat.
6. Aquila volat.
7. Cantat.
8. Antōnia ambulat.
9. Familia ōrat.
10. Saltat.

E. Prepositional Phrase Practice, p. 41
1. [In ecclēsiā] (Portia prays in the church.)
2. [In viā] (Antonia walks on the road.)
3. [ad ecclēsiam] (The maid walks to the church.)
4. [in villā] (Octavia prays in the villa.)
5. [in viā] (The family walks on the road.)
6. [In casā] (In the cottage Lucia dances.)
7. [in ecclēsiā] Maria prays in the church.
8. [In silvā] (The eagle flies in the forest.)

F. Missing Subjects, p. 41
1. Portia, Lūcia, Claudia, Octāvia, Maria, Antōnia, ancilla, fēmina, puella
2. aquila
3. Portia, Lūcia, Claudia, Octāvia, Maria, Antōnia, ancilla, fēmina, puella
4. Portia, Lūcia, Claudia, Octāvia, Maria, Antōnia, ancilla, fēmina, puella
5. Ancillæ, Fēminæ, Puellæ
6. Portia, Lūcia, Claudia, Octāvia, Maria, Antōnia, ancilla, fēmina, puella
7. Portia, Lūcia, Claudia, Octāvia, Maria, Antōnia
8. Ecclēsia, villa
9. Portia, Lūcia, Claudia, Octāvia, Maria, Antōnia, ancilla, fēmina, puella
10. Portia, Lūcia, Claudia, Octāvia, Maria, Antōnia, ancilla, fēmina, puella

G. Missing Verbs, p. 42
1. saltat, cantat, ōrat
2. volat
3. sunt
4. ambulat
5. est
6. sunt
7. ōrat
8. ambulat
9. cantat
10. est

H. Identify Sentence Elements, p. 42
1. <u>In the villa</u> Lucia sings. (prepositional phrase)
2. She dances. (intransitive verb)
3. <u>Maria and Portia</u> are maidservants. (compound subject)
4. The road <u>is</u> straight. (being verb)
5. The church is <u>new</u>. (predicate adjective)
6. <u>The eagle</u> is large. (subject)
7. She is <u>not</u> wealthy. (adverb)
8. Claudia <u>and</u> Octavia are girls. (conjunction)

Lesson Ten
A. Latin Noun Practice, p. 44
1. āra, āræ
2. columna, columnæ
3. familia, famīliæ
4. statua, statuæ

B. Grammar Questions, p. 44
1. plural
2. plural
3. subject
4. now
5. plural
6. singular

C. Adjective Phrases, p. 44
1. (tall column) singular
2. (pretty statue) singular
3. (tall columns) plural
4. (glorious windows) plural
5. (ancient church) singular
6. (splendid altar) singular
7. (glorious window) singular
8. (beautiful statues) plural
9. (ancient churches) plural
10. (splendid altars) plural

D. Subject-Verb Agreeement, p. 44
1. a. Puella ōrat in ecclēsiā. (The girl prays in the church.)
2. b. Lucīa et Portia sunt Rōmānæ. (Lucia and Octavia are Roman.)
3. b. Ancillæ laborant in villā. (The maidservants work in the villa.)
4. b. Familiae ambulant ad ecclēsiam. (The families walk to the church.)
5. a. Via est antīqua. (The road is ancient.)
6. a. In silvā aquila volat. (The eagle flies in the forest.)
7. a. In casā fēmina habitat. (The woman lives in the cottage.)
8. a. Alta columna stat. (The tall column stands.)

E. Matching, p. 45

1. D. ambulant (The women walk on the road.)
2. I. laborat (In the villa the maidservant works.)
3. E. ōrant (The families pray in the church.)
4. G. stant (The statues stand.)
5. B. laborant (The good maidservants work.)
6. F. habitant (Octavia and Claudia live in the villa.)
7. J. stat (The tall column stands.)
8. H. volant (The eagles fly.)
9. C. cantat (Portia sings in the cottage.)
10. A. volat (The eagle flies in the forest.)

F. Latin-to-English, p. 45

1. he, she, it stands
2. he, she, it prays
3. they live
4. he, she, it sings
5. he, she, it walks
6. they dance
7. he, she, it flies
8. they sing
9. he, she, it works
10. he, she, it lives
11. they sing
12. they work
13. they stand
14. he, she, it dances
15. they walk

G. Sentence Elements Practice, p. 45

1. Puella Christiāna [ad ecclēsiam] ambulat. (The Christian girl walks to the church.)
2. Fenēstræ glōriōsæ sunt [in ecclēsiā]. (The glorious windows are in the church.)
3. [In villā] ancilla bona lāborat. (The good maidservant works in the villa.)
4. Āra splendida [in ecclēsiā] stat. (A splendid altar stands in the church.)
5. [In silvā] aquilæ magnæ volant. (Great eagles fly in the forest.)

H. Missing Macrons, p. 46

1. āra glōriōsa (a glorious altar)
2. fenestra glōriōsa (a glorious window)
3. ecclēsia nova (the new church)
4. āra splendida (a splendid altar)
5. vīa Rōmāna (the Roman road)
6. ecclēsia antīqua (the ancient church)
7. fēmina Christiana (the Christian woman)
8. casa Rōmāna (Roman cottage)
9. silva antīqua (ancient forest)
10. puella Rōmāna (Roman girl)

I. Missing Adjectives, p. 46
1. magnæ (Large eagles fly.)
2. glōriōsæ (Glorious windows are in the church.)
3. Rōmānæ (Roman women walk to the villa.)
4. bona (The good maidservant works.)
5. opulenta (The wealthy family lives in the villa.)
6. bona (The good woman walks to the church.)
7. Altæ (Tall columns stand in the villa.)
8. pulchra (The pretty girl sings.)

J. Adjective Phrase Practice, p. 46
1. casa parva (the small cottage)
2. statua pulchra (the beautiful statue)
3. fenestra glōriōsa (glorious window)
4. alta columna (tall column)

Lesson Eleven
A. Predicate Nominatives or Adjectives?, p. 48
1. Fēmina is a predicate nominative. (Maria is a woman.)
2. Pæninsula is a predicate nominative. (Italy is a peninsula.)
3. Rōmānæ is a predicate adjective. (The women are Roman.)
4. Insula is a predicate nominative. (Sicily is an island.)
5. Parvæ is a predicate adjective. (The islands are small.)

B. Predicate Nominatives, p. 48
1. Lucīa est fēmina, ancilla, puella. (Lucia is a woman, maidservant, or girl.)
2. Ītalia nōn est insula. (Italy is not an island.)
3. Octāvia est fēmina, puella, or ancilla. (Octavia is a woman, girl or maidservant.)
4. Ītalia est pæninsula. (Italy is a peninsula.)
5. Sicilia est insula. (Sicily is an island.)

C. Predicate Adjectives, p. 48
1. nōta (Mount Aetna is famous.)
2. antīqua, magna, parva (The church is ancient, large, small.)
3. longa, antīqua (The road is long, ancient.)
4. longa, magna, parva (The peninsula is not long, large, small.)
5. Christiāna, parva, (The girl is Christian, small.)

D. Prepositional Phrase Practice, p. 48
1. B. near the island
2. E. near Italy
3. A. near the forest
4. C. near the cottage
5. F. near Sicily
6. D. near the peninsula

E. More Prepositional Phrases, p. 49

1. [Ad ecclēsiam] (The girls walk to the church.)
2. [Prope silvam] (Lucia walks near the forest.)
3. [ad ecclēsiam] (Maria and Portia walk to the church.)
4. [in villā] (Antonia lives in a villa.)
5. [In viā] (The families walk on the road.)
6. [In casā] (The girls dance in the cottage.)
7. [prope Ītaliam] (Sicily is near Italy.)
8. [prope silvam] (The eagles fly near the forest.)
9. [prope insulam] (The peninsula is near the island.)
10. [In ecclēsiā] (Tall columns stand in the church.)

F. Missing Predicate Adjectives, p. 49

1. nōtæ (The islands are famous.)
2. splendidæ (The windows are splendid.)
3. magna (The eagle is large.)
4. Rōmānæ (The maidservants are not Roman.)
5. recta (The road is not straight.)
6. antīqua (The forest is ancient.)
7. altæ (The columns are tall.)
8. glōriōsa (The altar is glorious.)

G. Missing Predicate Nominatives, p. 49

1. insula (Sicily is an island.)
2. ancillæ (Maria and Portia are maidservants.)
3. fēmina (Antōnia is a woman.)
4. ancilla (Claudia is not a maidservant.)
5. insula (Italy is not an island.)
6. puellæ (Octavia and Claudia are girls.)

H. Latin-to-English, p. 50

1. Near the forest an eagle flies.
2. The Christian churches are splendid.
3. In the church there are glorious windows.
4. The roads in Sicily are not long.
5. Roman roads are straight.
6. Sicilia is a famous island.
7. Sicily is a large island in Europe.
8. In the villa large columns stand.

I. Sentence Elements Practice, p. 50

1. intransitive verb (The girls walk to the church.)
2. subject (Mount Etna is famous.)
3. adjective (The good maidservant works.)
4. prepositional phrase (The splendid altar stands in the church.)
5. predicate adjective (The Roman road is straight.)
6. predicate nominative (Sicily is an island.)
7. adverb (Maria is not Roman.)

I. Sentence Elements Practice, p. 50 (continued)
8. conjunction (Lucia and Portia are Christian.)
9. being verb (Italy is a peninsula.)

Lesson Twelve
A. Adjective Phrase Practice, p. 51
1. Octavia is a good girl. (puella bona)
2. Lucia is a wealthy woman. (fēmina opulenta)
3. Italia is a large peninsula. (pæninsula magna)
4. There are splendid churches in Italy. (ecclēsiæ splendidæ)
5. Roman women walk on the road. (Fēminæ Rōmānæ)
6. There are glorious windows in the church. (Fenēstræ glōriōsæ)
7. A splendid altar is in the church. (āra splendida)
8. There are small islands near Italy. (Īnsulæ parvæ)
9. Italy is a famous peninsula. (pæninsula nōta)
10. Sicily is a large island. (insula magna)

B. Grammar Questions, p. 52
1. before
2. after
3. singular
4. plural
5. subject
6. nouns
7. adjectives
8. plural
9. **-a**
10. -æ
11. now
12. plural
13. singular
14. do not
15. intransitive

C. Subject-Verb Agreement, p. 52
1. b. ōrant (The women pray in the church.)
2. a. est (Claudia is Roman.)
3. a. habitat (The family lives in the cottage.)
4. b. laborant(The maidservants work in the country manor.)
5. a. volat (The eagle flies.)
6. b. stant (The columns in the church stand.)
7. b. saltant (the girls dance in the forest.)
8. a. est (Sicily is near Italy.)
9. a. stat (The altar stands in the church.)
10. b. sunt (The cottages are near the forest.)
11. a. cantat (Octāvia sings.)
12. a. est (Italy is not an island.)

D. Identification, p. 53

1. <u>Fenēstræ</u> (The <u>windows</u> are glorious.)
2. <u>Octāvia</u> (<u>Octavia</u> is a good girl.)
3. <u>Ītalia</u> (<u>Italy</u> is a peninsula.)
4. <u>Insulæ</u> (The islands are large.)
5. <u>Terra</u> (The land is ancient.)
6. <u>Ītalia</u> (Italy is a Christian country.)
7. <u>Stātuæ</u> (The statues are beautiful.)
8. <u>insulæ</u> (Many islands are famous.)
9. <u>Via</u> (The road is new.)
10. <u>Aquilæ</u> (The eagles are large.)

E. Subject / Verb Agreement, p. 53

1. est (The girl <u>is</u> Roman.)
2. sunt (The women <u>are</u> good.)
3. sunt (Claudia and Octave <u>are</u> not Christian.)
4. sunt (The families are wealthy.)
5. est (The window is new.)
6. est (The statue is ancient.)
7. est (Italy is a famous land.)
8. sunt (The roads are not straight.)
9. sunt (Portia and Maria are maidservants.)
10. est (The island is near Italy.)

F. Identification, p. 53

1. <u>habitat</u>	singular	(The family lives in Italy.)
2. <u>ōrant</u>	plural	(Women pray in the church.)
3. <u>ambulant</u>	plural	(Maria and Lucia walk.)
4. <u>cantat</u>	singular	(Claudia sings.)
5. <u>laborant</u>	plural	(In the villa the maidservants work.)

G. Identification, p. 54

1. <u>multæ ecclēsiae</u>	many churches	(There are many churches in Italy.)
2. <u>fēmina opulenta</u>	wealthy woman	(Antonia is not a wealthy woman.)
3. <u>pæninsula longa</u>	long peninsula	(Italy is a long peninsula.)
4. <u>insula nota</u>	famous island	(Sicily is a famous island.)
5. <u>puellæ Rōmānæ</u>	Roman girls	(They are Roman girls.)
6. <u>multæ aquilæ</u>	many eagles	(Many eagles fly in the forest.)
7. <u>terra antīqua</u>	ancient land	(It is an ancient country.)
8. <u>viæ longæ</u>	long roads	(There are no long roads in Sicily.)
9. <u>insula nōta</u>	famous island	(Sicily is a famous island.)
10. <u>puella Rōmāna</u>	Roman girl	(Octavia is a Roman girl.)

H. English-to-Latin, p. 54
1. multæ insulæ
2. multæ terræ
3. multæ pænīnsulæ
4. multæ aquilæ
5. multæ columnæ
6. multæ fenestræ
7. multæ puellæ
8. multæ fēminæ
9. multæ ecclēsiæ
10. multæ viæ

I. Missing Macrons, p. 54
1. terra antīqua (ancient country)
2. insula nōta (famous island)
3. via Rōmāna (Roman road)
4. pæninsula nōta (famous peninsula)
5. multæ ecclēsiæ (many churchess)
6. statua glōriōsa (glorious statue)
7. familia Christiāna (Christian family)
8. ecclēsia antīqua (ancient church)

Lessons 9-12 Review, p. 55
A. Grammar Review
1. Plural
2. Singular
3. adjective
4. singular
5. plural
6. Nouns
7. -a
8. -æ
9. declensions
10. feminine
11. subject
12. In
13. adverb
14. conjunction
15. preposition
16. prepositional phrase
17. after
18. must
19. do not
20. intransitive
21. plural
22. now
23. nominatives
24. adjectives
25. subjects

B. First Declension Noun Review, p. 56
1. maidservant, f.
2. eagle, f.
3. altar, f.
4. cottage, f.
5. column, f.
6. church, f.
7. family, f.
8. woman, f.
9. window, f.
10. island, f.
11. Italy, f.
12. Mt. Etna, f.
13. peninsula, f.
14. girl, f.
15. Sicily, f.
16. forest, f.
17. statue, f.
18. land, f.
19. road, f.
20. villa, f.

C. First Declension Adjective Review, p. 56

1. tall
2. old, ancient
3. good
4. Christian
5. glorious
6. long
7. large, great
8. many
9. new
10. wealthy, grand
11. small
12. pretty, beautiful
13. straight
14. Roman
15. splendid, shining

D. Intransitive Verbs Review, p. 57

1. she walks, singular
2. they walk, plural
3. she sings, singular
4. they sing, plural
5. she lives, singular
6. they live, plural
7. she works, singular
8. they work, plural
9. she prays, singular
10. they pray, plural
11. she dances, singular
12. they dance, plural
13. she, it stands, singular
14. they stand, plural
15. she, it flies, singular
16. they fly, plural

E. Being Verbs Review, p. 57

1. she is, singular
2. they are, plural

F. Preposition Review, p. 57

1. in, on, upon
2. to, toward
3. near

G. Conjunction Review, p. 57

1. and

H. Adverb Review, p. 57

1. not

I. Prepositional Phrases Review, p. 57

1. in the villa
2. in the cottage
3. to the church
4. near the island

J. Forming Nominative Plurals, p. 58

1. terræ
2. fenestræ
3. columnæ
4. viæ
5. īnsulæ

K. Subjects and Verbs, p. 58

1. yes
2. Yes
3. Yes
4. Yes
5. Yes

L. Subject-Verb Agreement, p. 58

1. stat
2. est
3. habitat
4. volat
5. sunt

M. Predicate Nominative/Adjective Identification, p. 58

1. predicate nominative
2. predicate adjective
3. predicate adjective
4. predicate nominative
5. predicate adjective

N. Prepositional Phrase Identification, p. 59

1. The girl lives in the small cottage. [in casā parvā]
2. Tall columns stand in the church. [In ecclēsiā]
3. The eagle flies over the forest. [prope silvam]
4. To the villa she walks. [Ad villam]
5. The girls walk on the long road. [in viā longā]

O. Matching, p. 59

1. E. the splendid altar
2. B. glorious windows
3. G. many islands
4. K. an ancient land
5. M. a great forest
6. O. new roads
7. I. straight road
8. N. opulent (grand) villas
9. J. Roman girl
10. A. the large eagles
11. H. a long island
12. D. the famous peninsula
13. F. beautiful statues
14. C. a good maidservant
15. L. the ancient church

P. Sentence Translation, p. 59
1. They sing and dance.
2. The roads in Sicily are not long.
3. Italy is an ancient land.
4. The forests are large.
5. The family lives on the peninsula.

Q. Subject Identification, p. 60
1. The girl walks on the road. <u>puella</u>
2. The road is not straight. <u>via</u>
3. Eagles fly. <u>aquilæ</u>
4. Italy is a peninsula. <u>Ītalia</u>
5. Sicily is an island. <u>Sicilia</u>
6. The maids are not Roman. <u>Ancillæ</u>
7. Mary and Lucia sing. <u>Maria et Lūcia</u>
8. Lucia walks to the church. <u>Lūcia</u>
9. The altar is splendid. <u>Āra</u>
10. The eagle flies. <u>Aquila</u>

R. Intransitive Verbs, p. 60
1. The maid works in the cottage. <u>laborat</u> (singular)
2. The eagles fly in the forest. <u>volant</u> (plural)
3. Lucia sings. <u>cantat</u> (singular)
4. The column stands. <u>stat</u> (singular)
5. The families pray in the church. <u>ōrant</u> (plural)

S. Proofreading, p. 60
1. The woman walks. ~~fæmina~~ fēmina
2. The eagle flies near the cottage. ~~aqila~~ aquila
3. Italia is an ancient land. ~~Italiat~~ Ītalia
4. A tall column stands in the church. ~~colomna~~ columna
5. There are many churches in Italy. ~~eclesiæ~~ ecclēsiæ
6. The villas are splendid. ~~eunt~~ sunt
7. She walks to the church. ~~aimbulat~~ ambulat
8. The road is straight. ~~rocta~~ recta
9. Sicily is a large island. ~~mana~~ magna
10. The girls are Roman. ~~pullæ~~ puellæ

Lesson Thirteen
A. Grammar Questions, p. 62
1. before
2. after
3. singular
4. plural
5. subject
6. nominatives
7. adjectives

B. Adjective Phrases, p. 62
1. I. famous peninsula
2. F. Christian women
3. N. splendid churches
4. H. glorious window
5. O. small cottage
6. J. many islands
7. L. beautiful statue
8. B. ancient lands
9. D. good girl
10. E. ancient church
11. A. many lands
12. C. Christian family
13. K. wealthy villa
14. M. small forest
15. G. long roads

C. Predicate Nominatives or Adjectives?, p. 62
1. The altar is <u>large</u>. predicate adjective
2. Italy is a <u>peninsula</u>. predicate nominative
3. Mt. Etna is <u>famous</u>. predicate adjective
4. Sicily is an <u>island</u>. predicate nominative
5. The forest is <u>ancient</u>. predicate adjective

D. Missing Prepositional Phrases, p. 63
1. The girls walk to the church. (ad ecclēsiam)
2. The maidservant work in the villa. (in villā)
3. The eagles fly near the forest. (prope silvam)
4. The eagle flies over the forest. (super silvam
5. The island is near Italy. (prope Ītaliam)
6. The family lives in the cottage. (in casā)
7. The maidservants walk to the villa. (ad villam)
8. Lucia dances near the cottage. (prope casam)
9. In the church the women pray. (in ecclēsiā)

E. Prepositional Phrases, p. 63
1. M. in silvīs
2. O. in viā longā
3. L. in casīs
4. B. super silvās
5. J. prope ecclēsiam
6. A. in ecclēsiā antīquā
7. N. in casā parvā
8. K. in viā rectā
9. F. super silvam
10. C. in Ītaliā
11. E. prope pæninsulam
12. D. ad insulam
13. G. ad ecclēsiās
14. H. prope silvam
15. I. prope āram splendidam

F. Sentence Elements, p. 64
1. preposition
2. adverb
3. intransitive verb
4. predicate nominative
5. subject
6. being verb
7. conjunction
8. object of preposition
9. predicate adjective
10. adjective

G. Missing Subjects, p. 64
1. Maria et Lūcia
2. Viæ
3. aquila
4. Sicilia
5. Mons Ætna
6. Ancilla
7. fēmina
8. puella
9. Ecclēsiæ
10. Aquilæ
11. Claudia
12. puellæ
13. Fēminæ
14. fenestræ
15. columnæ

Lesson Fourteen
A. Adjective Phrase Practice, p. 66
1. columbæ speciōsæ (the beautiful doves)
2. famīliæ Christiānæ (Christian familie)
3. ancillæ bonæ (the good maidservants)
4. fenestræ glōriōsæ (glorious windows)
5. āræ splendidæ (splendid altars)
6. altæ columnæ (tall columns)
7. rosæ rubræ (red roses)
8. casæ parvæ (small cottages)

B. Proofreading, p. 66
1. There are red roses near the cottage. ~~sont~~ sunt
2. Lucia lives in the small cottage. ~~haebitat~~ habitat
3. Italy is an ancient land. ~~tera~~ terra
4. She prays in the splendid church. ~~eclesia~~ ecclēsiā
5. There are many churches. ~~meltæ~~ Multæ
6. A tall column stands in the church. ~~collummna~~ columna

C. Grammar Questions, p. 66
1. singular
2. plural
3. subject
4. before
5. after
6. singular
7. plural
8. nominatives
9. adjectives

D. Missing Adjectives, p. 67
1. The <u>famous</u> island is Sicily. nōta
2. <u>White</u> roses are near the cottage. albæ
3. A <u>large</u> eagle flies in the forest. magna
4. Maria is not a <u>Roman</u> girl. Rōmāna
5. They are not <u>straight</u> roads. rectæ
6. The <u>ancient</u> forest is in Italy. antīqua
7. The <u>beautiful</u> dove coos. speciōsa
8. <u>Tall</u> columns stnd in the church. Altæ
9. <u>Christian</u> families pray. Christiānæ
10. She is a <u>good</u> woman. bona
11. Italia is an <u>ancient</u> land. antīqua
12. Sicily is a <u>large</u> island. magna
13. The <u>good</u> girls walk on the road. bonæ
14. There are <u>glorious</u> windows in the villa. glōriōsæ
15. There is a <u>splendid</u> altar in the church. splendida

E. Prepositional Phrase Practice, p. 67

1. E. in casīs
2. I. super silvās
3. G. ad ecclēsiam
4. M. super ecclēsiās
5. L. in silvā
6. O. prope villam
7. B. in viā
8. A. in silvīs
9. D. ad casās
10. N. in ecclēsiīs
11. F. prope insulam
12. H. super terrās
13. K. in villīs
14. C. ad īnsulās
15. J. prope pæninsulam

F. Sentence Elements Practice, p. 68

1. The roses <u>are</u> red. being verb
2. The <u>forest</u> is dense. subject
3. The girl <u>dances</u> near the cottage. intransitive verb
4. Women sing <u>in</u> the church. preposition
5. Italy is a <u>peninsula</u>. predicate nominative
6. Claudia <u>and</u> Octavia are girls. conjunction
7. Doves coo in the <u>forest</u>. object of preposition
8. Sicily is <u>not</u> a peninsula. adverb
9. The church is <u>famous</u>. predicate adjective
10. <u>Many</u> roses are near the cottage. adjective

G. Sentence Translation, p. 68

1. Beautiful doves coo.
2. The roses are red and white.
3. Italy is a famous land.
4. The forests are dense.
5. Families live in the cottages.
6. A good girl prays in the church.
7. Tall columns stand.
8. They are not wealthy.

Lesson Fifteen
A. Subject/Verb Agreement, p. 70
1. a. In terrā agricola arat. (The farmer plows on the land.)
2. b. Āgricolæ arant. (The farmers plow.)
3. b. Aquilæ super silvam volant. (The eagles fly over the woods.)
4. a. Aquila volat. (The eagle flies.)
5. a. Colūmba murmurat. (The dove murmurs.)
6. b. In silvā columbæ murmurant. (In the forest, the doves murmur.)
7. b. Puellæ in silvā saltant. (The girls dance in the forest.)
8. a. Puella saltat. (The girl dances.)
9. a. Āra in ecclēsiā stat. (The altar stands in the church.)
10. b. columnæ stant. (The columns stand.)
11. b. Incolæ in silvā indāgant. (The inhabitants hunt in the forest.)
12. a. Īncola indāgat. (The inhabitant hunts.)

B. Identifying Feminine and Masculine Nouns, p. 70
1. statue (feminine)
2. inhabitant (masculine)
3. maidservant (feminine)
4. eagle (feminine)
5. window (feminine)
6. farmer (masculine)
7. altar (feminine)
8. rose (feminine
9. forest (feminine)
10. dove (feminine)
11. column (feminine)
12. church (feminine)
13. patriarch (masculine)
14. cottage (feminine)
15. girl (feminine)
16. island (feminine)
17. peninsula (feminine)

C. Identification, p. 71
1. The girl is Roman. (est)
2. The women are good. (sunt)
3. Claudia and Octavia are not Christian. (sunt)
4. He is a farmer. (est)
5. They are maidservants. (sunt)
6. The patriarch is in the church. (est)
7. They are inhabitants. (sunt)
8. It is a red rose. (est)
9. The column is tall. (est)
10. Italy is an ancient land. (est)

D. Identification, p. 71

1. The inhabitants <u>live</u> on the islands. (habitant) (plural)
2. The eagle flies over the forest. (volat) (singular)
3. The patriarch prays in the church. (ōrat) (singular)
4. The farmer plows. (arat) (singular)
5. The inhabitants hunt. (indāgant) (plural)
6. Lucia prays. (ōrat) (singular)
7. In the villas they work. (laborant) (plural)
8. She sings. (cantat) (singular)
9. A beautiful statue stands in the villa. (stat) (singular)
10. Doves coo. (murmurant) (plural)

E. Identification, p. 71

1. The <u>beautiful doves</u> murmur.
2. A <u>large eagle</u> flies.
3. They are <u>glorious windows</u>.
4. <u>Tall columns</u> stand.
5. <u>Dense forests</u> are not on the island.
6. Near the cottage are <u>red roses</u>.
7. A <u>good woman</u> walks on the road.
8. <u>Many girls</u> sing.

F. Identification, p. 72

1. The women walk <u>to the cottages</u>. (ad casās)
2. The maidservants work <u>in the villas</u>. (in villīs)
3. Eagles fly <u>over the forests</u>. (super silvās)
4. Statues stand <u>near the villas</u>. (prope villās)
5. Italy is <u>near the islands</u>. (prope īnsulās)
6. The inhabitants live <u>in cottages</u>. (in casīs)
7. A farmer plows <u>on the land</u>. (in terrā)
8. Inhabitants hunt <u>in the forests</u>. (in silvīs)
9. Patriarchs pray <u>in the churches</u>. (in ecclēsiīs)
10. The farmer walks <u>on the road</u>. (in viā)
11. Roses are <u>near the cottage</u>. (prope casam)
12. The eagle flies <u>above the land</u>. (super terram)

G. Missing Macrons, p. 72

1. ecclēsia parva (small church)
2. multæ fēminæ (many women)
3. villa antīqua (old villa)
4. pæninsula nōta (famous peninsula)
5. statua glōriōsa (glorious statue)
6. fēminæ Christiānæ (Christian women)
7. familia Rōmāna (a Roman family)
8. āra splendida (splendid altar)
9. fenestra gōriōsa (glorious window)
10. silvæ antīquæ (old forests)

Lesson Sixteen
A. Matching, p. 74
1. C. blue water
2. J. a beautiful life
3. M. straight roads
4. I. red roses
5. D. large eagle
6. N. a glorious window
7. H. white doves
8. E. small cottages
9. A. a good maidservant
10. F. Roman women
11. O. white boats
12. G. long shore
13. K. dense forest
14. B. splendid church
15. L. tall columns

B. Prepositional Phrases, p. 74
1. The boats are [in the blue water].
2. Straight roads are [in Italy].
3. White roses are [near the cottage].
4. Eagles fly [over the forests].
5. Farmers plow [on the land].
6. The island is [near Italy].
7. Wealthy families live [in the splendid villas].
8. The splendid altar stands [in the church].
9. Sailors are [in the boats].
10. Girls walk [to the church].
11. Doves coo [in the dense forest].
12. A girl dances [on the long shore].
13. Sailors live [in the cottages].
14. An eagle flies [over the water].
15. Maidservants walk [to the villas].

C. Subject -Verb Agreement, p. 75
1. A tall column stands in the villa. (stat)
2. The windows are glorious. (sunt)
3. The farmers plow on the land. (arant)
4. Eagles fly in the forests (volant)
5. The water is blue. (est)
6. Sailors sail on the water. (nāvigant)
7. The boat is white. (est)
8. The girl walks on the long shore. (ambulat)
9. Women sing. (cantant)
10. The patriarch prays. (ōrat)

D. Missing Predicate Nominatives, p. 75
1. Maria et Lūcia sunt puellæ. (Maria and Lucia are girls.)
2. Ītalia est pæninsula. (Italy is a peninsula.)
3. Claudia est fēmina. (Claudia is a woman.)
4. Sicilia est insula. (Sicily is an island.)
5. Portia est puella. (Portia is a girl.)

E. Missing Predicate Adjectives, p. 75
1. Colūmbæ sunt speciōsæ. (The doves are beautiful.)
2. Terra est antīqua. (The land is ancient.)
3. Nāviculæ sunt albæ. (The boats are white.)
4. Rōsæ sunt rubræ. (Roses are red.)
5. Ara est splendida. (The altar is splendid.)
6. Ecclēsia est magna. (The church is large.)
7. Vita est speciōsa. (Life is beautiful.)
8. Viæ sunt rectæ. (Roads are straight.)
9. Aquilæ sunt magnæ. (The eagles are large.)
10. Aqua est cærulea. (Water is blue.)

F. Intransitive Verbs, p. 76
1. Inhabitants <u>hunt</u> in the forest. (<u>indāgant</u>) (plural)
2. The eagle <u>flies</u> over the land. (<u>volat</u>) (singular)
3. Patriarchs <u>sing</u> in the churches. (<u>cantant</u>) (plural)
4. Tall columns <u>stand</u>. (<u>stant</u>) (plural)
5. The poet <u>sings</u> in the splendid villa. (<u>cantat</u>) (singular)
6. They <u>swim</u> in the blue water. (<u>natant</u>) (plural)
7. The dove <u>coos</u>. (<u>murmurat</u>) (singular)
8. The sailor <u>sails</u> in the water. (<u>nāvigat</u>) (singular)
9. Farmers <u>plow</u>. (<u>arant</u>) (plural)
10. A small girl <u>dances</u>. (<u>saltat</u>) (singular)

G. Identify Sentence Elements, p. 76
1. In the church the patriarcha <u>sings</u>. (intransitive verb)
2. Life in Italy is <u>beautiful</u>. (adjective)
3. The roads are <u>not</u> straight. (adverb)
4. The water <u>is</u> blue. (being verb)
5. The <u>farmer</u> plows. (subject)
6. Eagles fly <u>over</u> the forests. (object of preposition)
7. The roses are <u>near</u> the cottage. (preposition)
8. Octavia is a <u>woman</u>. (predicate nominative)
9. The new villa is <u>splendida</u>. (predicate nominative)
10. Maria <u>and</u> Lucia are maidservants. (conjunction)

Lessons 13-16, Review, p. 77
A. Grammar Review, p. 77

1. Plural nouns refer to more than one person, place or thing.
2. Singular nouns refer to one person, place or thing.
3. An adjective is a word which describes a noun or pronoun.
4. Est is a singular being verb.
5. Sunt is a plural being verb.
6. Nouns are words that name persons, places or things.
7. The first declension nominative singular ending is -a.
8. The first declension nominative plural ending is -æ.
9. Latin nouns are placed in groups called declensions.
10. Most first declension nouns are feminine.
11. The subject is the person, place or thing the sentence is about.
12. In may be translated as in, on, or upon.
13. Nōn is an adverb.
14. Et is a conjunction which joins words together.
15. In is a preposition showing a relationship between words.
16. First declension masculine nouns in the nominative case do end in -a in the singular and -æ in the plural, just like first declension feminine nouns.
17. Adjectives of quality are usually placed after the nouns they modify.
18. Latin adjectives must agreee with the nouns they modify in case, number and gender.
19. Intransitive verbs do not require an object to complete their meaning.
20. Ōrat, cantat and ambulat are intransitive verbs.
21. Third person plural verbs end in -nt.
22. Present tense means the action is happening now.
23. Predicate nominatives are nouns which follow being verbs and rename the subject.
24. Predicate adjectives are adjectives which follow a being verb and rename the subject.
25. Third person means the subject is being spoken about.

B. First Declension Nouns, p. 78

1. water (feminine)
2. eagle (feminine)
3. altar (feminine)
4. land (feminine)
5. dove (feminine)
6. window (feminine)
7. shore (feminine)
8. boat (feminine)
9. rose (feminine)
10. life (feminine)
11. farmer (masculine)
12. sailor (masculine)
13. inhabitant (masculine)
14. patriarch (masculine)
15. poet (masculine)

C. First and Second Declension Adjectives, p. 78

1. white
2. tall
3. ancient
4. blue
5. dense
6. large, great
7. many
8. new
9. wealthy, grand
10. straight
11. red
12. beautiful

D. Being Verbs, p. 79

1. is
2. are

E. Prepositions Review, p. 79

1. in, on, upon
2. to, toward
3. near
4. over, above

F. Conjunction Review, p. 79

1. and

G. Adverb, p. 79

1. not

H. Prepositional Phrases Review, p. 79

1. in villā (in the villa)
2. in casā (in the cottage)
3. ad ecclēsiam (to the church)
4. prope insulam (near the island)
5. prope Ītaliam (near Italy)
6. prope casam (near the cottage)
7. in terrā (on the land)
8. in ōrā (on the shore)
9. in aquā (in, on the water)
10. in villā splēndidā (in the splendid villa)
11. in casā parva (in the small cottage)
12. in silvā densā (in the dense forest)
13. super silvās (above the forests)
14. in casīs (in the cottages)
15. in nāviculīs (in, on the boats)
16. in aquā cæruleā (in, on the blue water)

I. Intransitive Verbs Review, p. 80

1. arat (he, she, it plows)
2. arant (they plow)
3. cantat (he, she, it sings)
4. cantant (they sing)
5. habitat (he, she, it lives)
6. habitant (they live)
7. indāgat (he, she, it hunts)
8. indāgant (they hunt)
9. murmurat (he, she, it murmurs, coos)
10. murmurant (they murmur, coo)
11. natat (he, she, it swims)
12. natant (they swim)
13. nāvigat (he, she, it sails)
14. nāvigant (they sail)
15. saltat (he, she, it dances)
16. saltant (they dance)
17. stat (he, she, it stands)
18. stant (they stand)
19. volat (he, she, it flies)
20. volant (they fly)

Part II. Practical Application, p. 81
J. Forming Nominative Plurals

1. fenestra, fenestræ (window, windows)
2. columba, columbæ (dove, doves)
3. nauta, nautæ (sailor, sailors)
4. insula, insulæ (island, islands)

K. Subjects and Verbs, p. 81

1. Yes, <u>Colūmbæ</u> and <u>murmurant</u> are both plural. (Doves murmur in the woods.)
2. No, <u>agricolæ</u> is plural, and <u>laborat</u>is singular. Should be: In terrā agricolæ laborant. (On the land farmers plow.)
3. No, <u>Nautæ</u> is plural, and <u>est</u> is singular. Should be: Nautae sunt in nāviculīs. (Sailors are in the boats.)
4. Yes, <u>Vita</u> and <u>est</u> are both singular. (Life is beautiful in ancient Italy.)
5. Yes, <u>Puellæ</u> and <u>natant</u> are both plural. (The girls swim in the water.)

L. Subject/Verb Agreement, p. 81

1. Nautæ nāvigant. (Sailors sail.)
2. Fenestra est glōriōsa. (The window is glorious.)
3. In orā puellæ saltant. (The girls dance on the shore.
4. Super silvās aquila volat. (Over the woods the eagle flies.)
5. columnæ sunt altæ. (The columns are tall.)

M. Predicate Nominative/Adjective Identification, p. 81

1. The water is blue. (Cærulea is a predicate adjective modifying aqua.)
2. The rose is white. (Alba is a predicate adjective modifying rosa.)
3. Feminæ sunt opulentæ. (Opulentae is a predicate adjective modifying fēminae.)
4. Portia is a maidservant. (Ancilla is a predicate nominative giving more information about Portia.)
5. The sailor is an inhabitant. (Incola is a predicate nominative giving information about nauta.)
6, Columns are tall. (Altæ is a predicate adjective modifying columnæ.)
7. Sicily is an island. (Insula is a predicate nominative modifying Sicilia.)
8. Italy is a peninsula. (Pæninsula is a predicate nominative modifying Ītalia.)
9. The family is Roman. (Rōmāna is a predicate adjective modifying familia.)
10. The lands are ancient. (Antīquæ is a predicate adjective modifying terræ.)

N. Prepositional Phrase Identification, p. 82
1. The girl lives <u>in the small cottage</u>. (in casā parvā)
2. Tall columns stand <u>in the church</u>. (in ecclēsiā)
3. The eagle flies <u>over the forests.</u> (super silvās)
4. <u>In the dense forest</u> doves murmur. (in silvā densā)
5. <u>On the long road</u> maidservants walk. (In viā longā)

O. Matching, p. 82
1. M. red rose (rosa rubra)
2. O. glorious windows (fenēstræ glōriōsæ)
3. H. splendid altar (āra splendida)
4. K. Roman girls (puellæ Rōmānæ)
5. C. a dense forest (silva densa)
6. A. the blue water (aqua cærulea)
7. I. straight roads (viæ rectæ)
8. N. new villas (villæ novæ)
9. F. beautiful doves (columbæ speciōsæ)
10. E. a large eagle (aquila magna)
11. B. white boats (nāviculæ albæ)
12. G. many sailors (Multæ nautæ)
13. J. beautiful statue (statua pulchra)
14. D. famous peninsula (pæninsula nōta)
15. L. ancient land (terra antīqua)

P. Sentence Translation, p. 82
1. They sing and pray in the church.
2. The roads in Sicily are not long.
3. Italy is a Christian land.
4. The roses are white and red.
5. The inhabitants live on the peninsula.

Q. Prepositional Phrase Identification, p. 83
1. The boats <u>in the water</u> are blue. (in aquā)
2. There are not straight roads <u>in Sicily</u>. (in Siciliā)
3. Red roses are <u>near the cottage</u>. (prope casam)
4. Eagles fly <u>over the forest</u>. (super silvam)
5. The farmer plows <u>on the land</u>. (in terrā)
6. The island is <u>near Italy</u>. (prope Ītaliam)
7. A wealthy family lives <u>in the splendid villa</u>. (in villā splēndidā)
8. Tall columns stand <u>in the church</u>. (in ecclēsiā)
9. The sailor is <u>in the boat</u>. (in nāviculā)
10. The girls walk <u>to the church</u>. (ad ecclēsiam)

R. Intransitive Verbs, p. 83

1. The inhabitant hunts in the forest. (indāgat) (singular)
2. The eagles fly over the forests. (volant) (plural)
3. The patriarch sing in the church. (cantat) (singular)
4. Tall columns stand. (stant) (plural)
5. The poet sings in the splendid villa. (cantat) (singular)

S. Proofreading, p. 42

1. Agrīcola arat. (The farmer plows.) (Agrecola)
2. Prope casam columbae murmurant. (Near the cottage the doves murmur.) (colmbae)
3. In Sicīliā est Mons Ætna. (Mount Etna is in Sicily.) (oest)
4. Fēminæ bonæ ambulant. (The good women walk.) (ambulornt)
5. Sunt multæ ecclēsiæ in Ītaliā. (There are many churches in Italy.) (ecclisiae)
6. Rosæ sunt albæ et rubræ. (The roses are white and red.) (rubraie)

GLOSSARY OF GRAMMATICAL TERMS

adjective word which describes a noun or pronoun and agrees with the noun in number and gender

adjective of quality an adjective which answers the question 'what kind of?'Adjectives of quality generally follow directly *after* the nouns they modify

adjective of quantity an adjective which answers the question 'how many?' Adjectives of quantitity generally follow directly *before* the nouns they modify

adverb part of speech used to modify a verb or another adverb, e.g., *nunc, subito, non*

being verb indicates the existence of a state or condition, usually followed by a predicate complement

case the six particular forms of nouns and pronouns, and the adjectives that modify them. The six cases used in Latin are nominative, genitive, dative, accusative, ablative and vocative.

conjunction word used to connect other parts of speech, e.g., *et, quoque*

declension a group of nouns classified according to endings. There are five declensions in Latin.

ending the prescribed noun suffix, or ending of each case in every declension

feminine nouns belonging in this category are considered to be female

first declension nouns ending in **-a** in the nominative singular and in **-ae** in the genitive singular; mostly feminine in gender with a few common masculine nouns

first and second declension adjectives adjectives which use the endings of first and second declension masculine, feminine and neuter nouns. Their endings are listed as **-us, -a, -um** in a dictionary entry.

first person verbs or pronouns in first person mean the subject is speaking

gender every Latin noun is classified either as **feminine**, **masculine** or **neuter**

intransitive verbs verbs which do not require an object to complete their meaning

masculine nouns belonging in this category are considered to be male

neuter nouns belonging in this category are considered to be neither male nor female

nominative case used to denote subjects, predicate nominatives and predicate adjectives

noun part of speech which names a person, place, thing or idea.

125

number quantity of a noun, adjective or the subject of a verb; may be singular (one) or plural (more than one)

plural more than one; refers to nouns, adjectives or verbs

predicate adjective a predicate complement which is an adjective describing the subject; follows a being verb

predicate complement noun which follows a being verb

predicate nominative a predicate complement which is a noun or pronoun describing or renaming the subject in some way; follows a being verb

preposition word used to describe a relationship between other words in a sentence. A preposition introduces a prepositional phrase. Example: in, on, after, behind, over

present tense refers to action in the current time

root noun stem to which endings are attached. The root is found by removing the genitive singular ending from a noun. The letters that remain are the root stem.

second person verbs or pronouns in second person mean the subect is being spoken to

singular one; refers to nouns, adjectives and verbs

subject the noun that is the person, place, thing or idea that is doing or being something

third person verbs or pronouns in third person mean the subject is being talked about

verb a word showing an action or indicating the existence of a state or condition

First Declension Feminine Nouns	First Declension Feminine Nouns	First Declension Feminine Nouns
First Declension Feminine Adjectives	First Declension Feminine Adjectives	First Declension Feminine Adjectives
Being Verbs	Being Verbs	Being Verbs
Intransitive Verbs	Intransitive Verbs	Intransitive Verbs
Prepositions	Prepositions	Prepositions
Prepositional Phrases	Prepositional Phrases	Prepositional Phrases
Adverbs	Adverbs	Adverbs
Conjunctions	Conjunctions	Conjunctions
Grammar Definitions	Grammar Definitions	Grammar Definitions
Latin Prayers	Latin Prayers	Latin Prayers
First Declension Feminine Nouns	First Declension Feminine Nouns	First Declension Feminine Nouns
First Declension Feminine Adjectives	First Declension Feminine Adjectives	First Declension Feminine Adjectives
Being Verbs	Being Verbs	Being Verbs
Intransitive Verbs	Intransitive Verbs	Intransitive Verbs
Prepositions	Prepositions	Prepositions
Prepositional Phrases	Prepositional Phrases	Prepositional Phrases
Adverbs	Adverbs	Adverbs
Conjunctions	Conjunctions	Conjunctions
Grammar Definitions	Grammar Definitions	Grammar Definitions
Latin Prayers	Latin Prayers	Latin

Made in the USA
Monee, IL
14 September 2023

42577357R00072